I0468654

TRANQUIL MIND

Botanicals

Marlene Cooper

Copyright © 2016 Marlene Cooper

All rights reserved.

ISBN:153031805X
ISBN-13: 978-1530318056

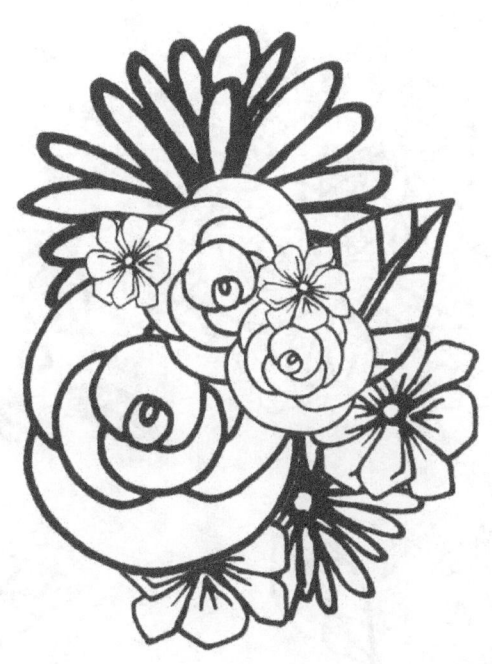

To Sean, my guardian angel.

To my mother who never allowed my art supplies to run dry.

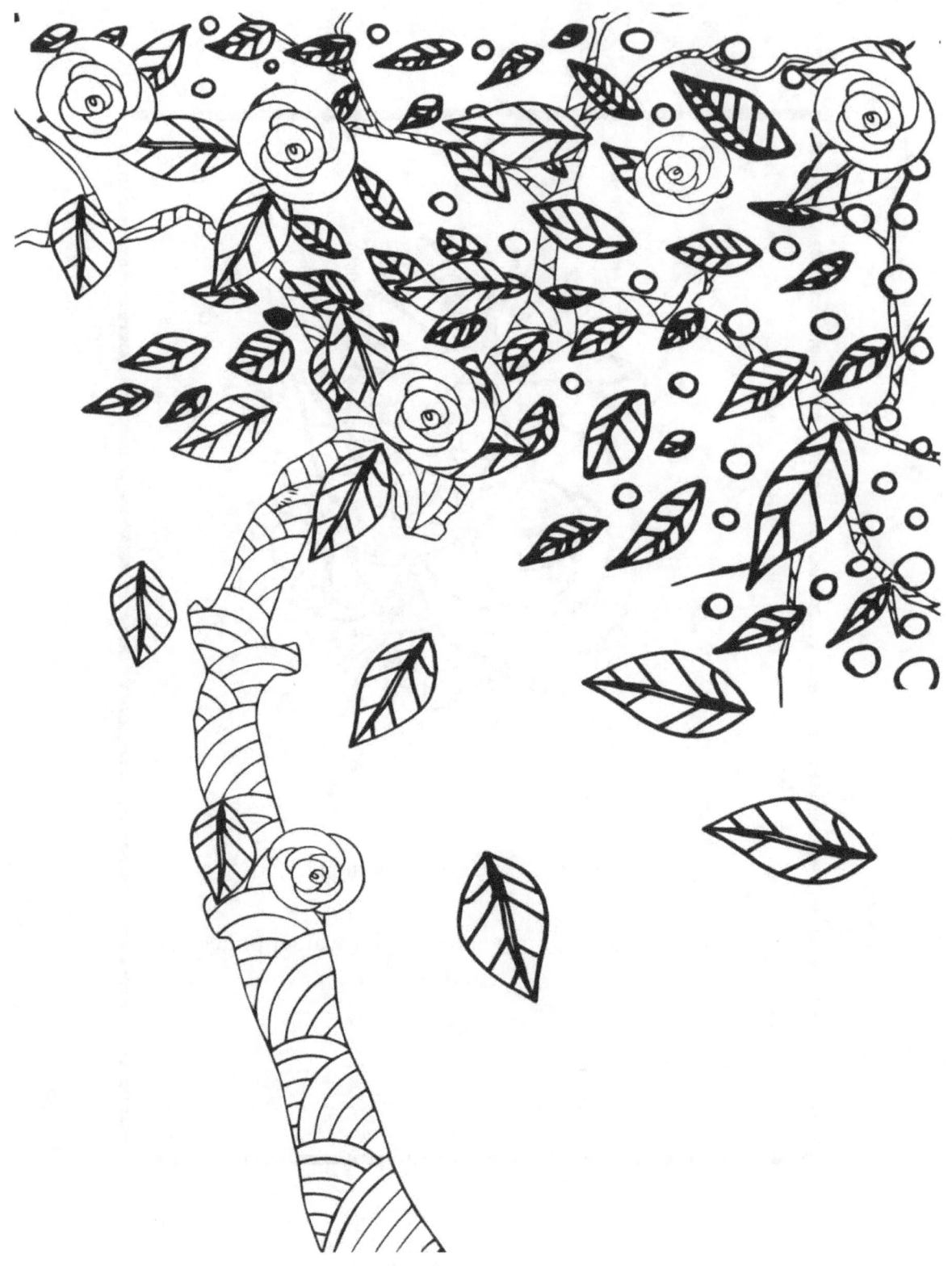

4

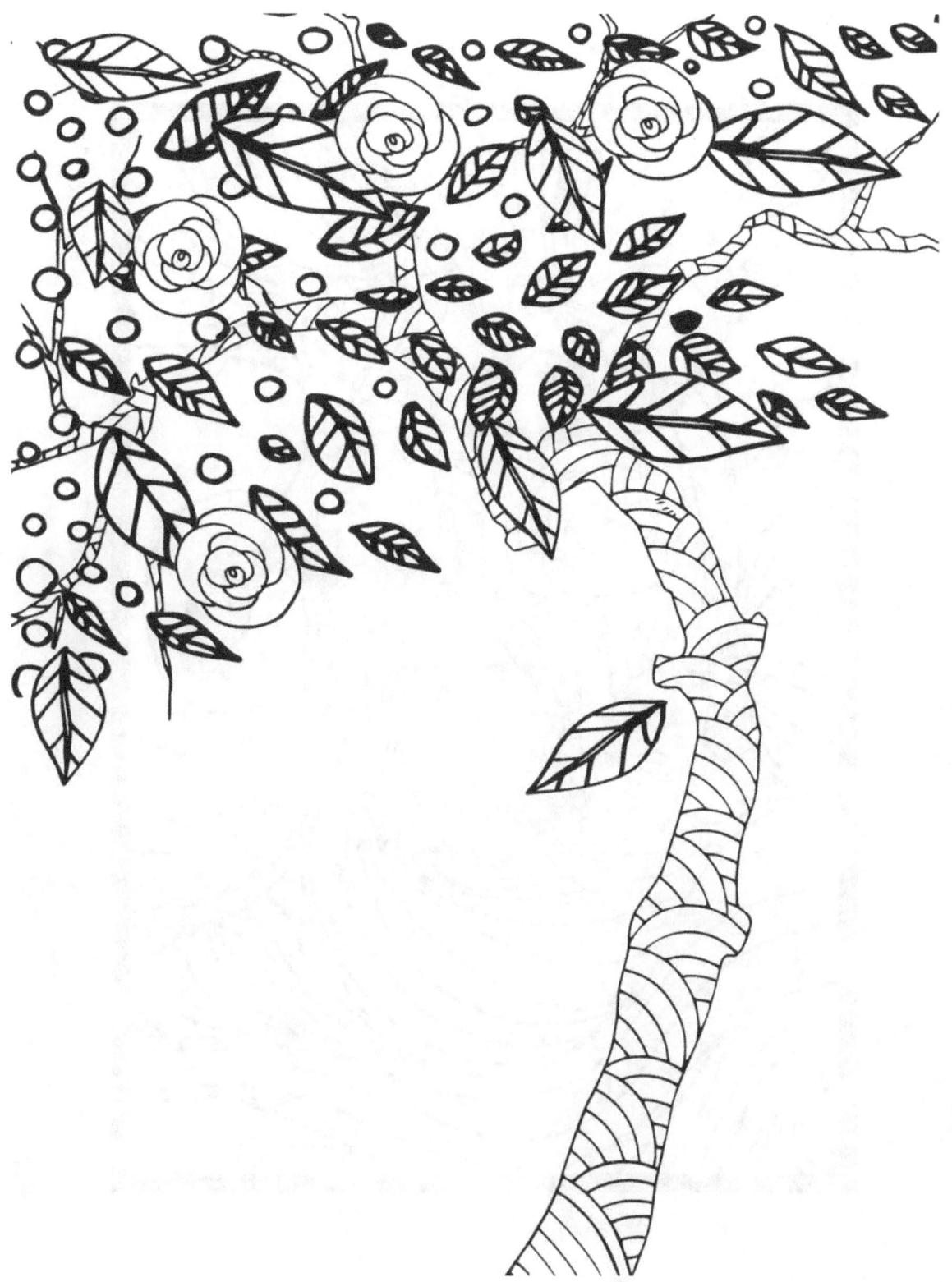

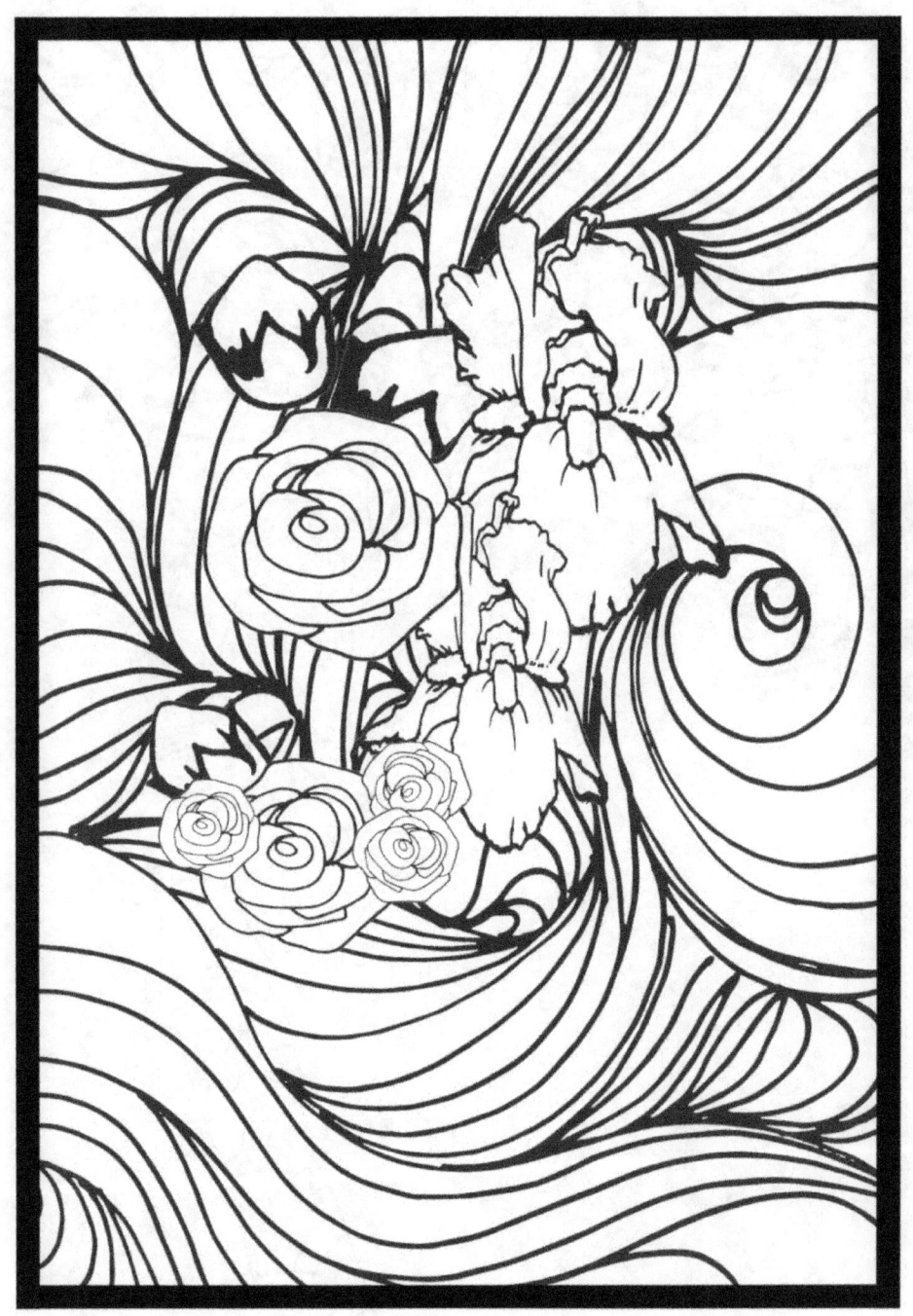

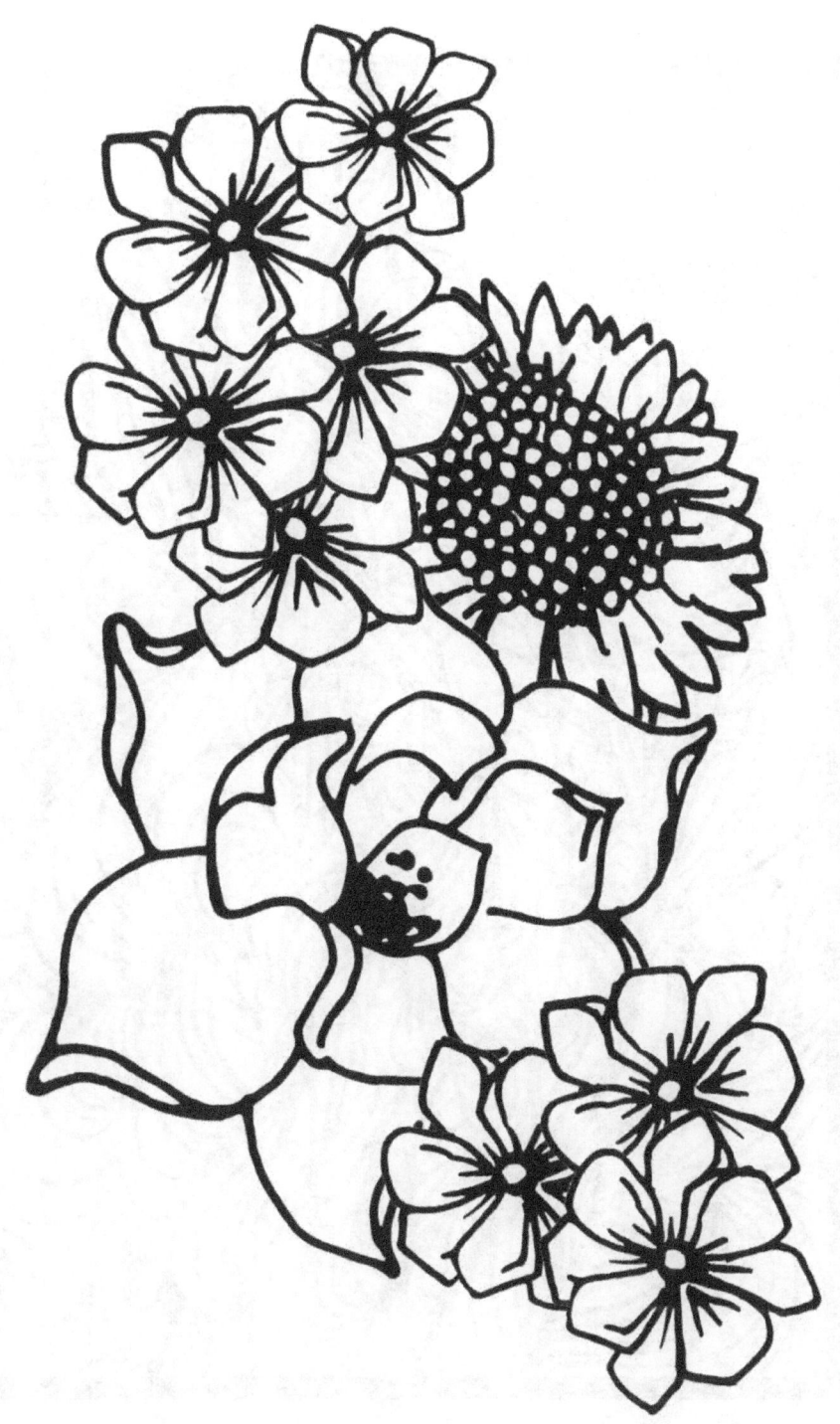

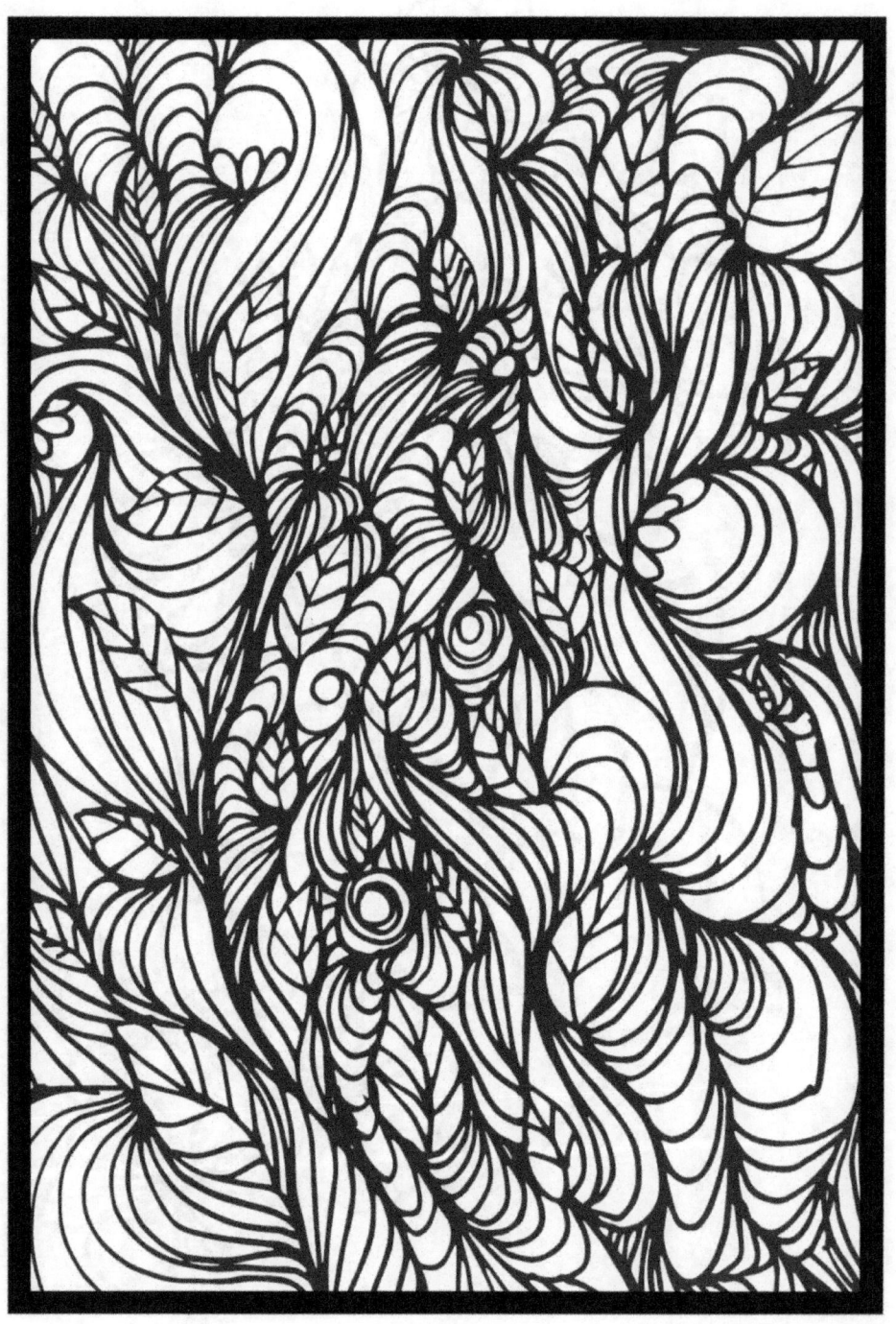

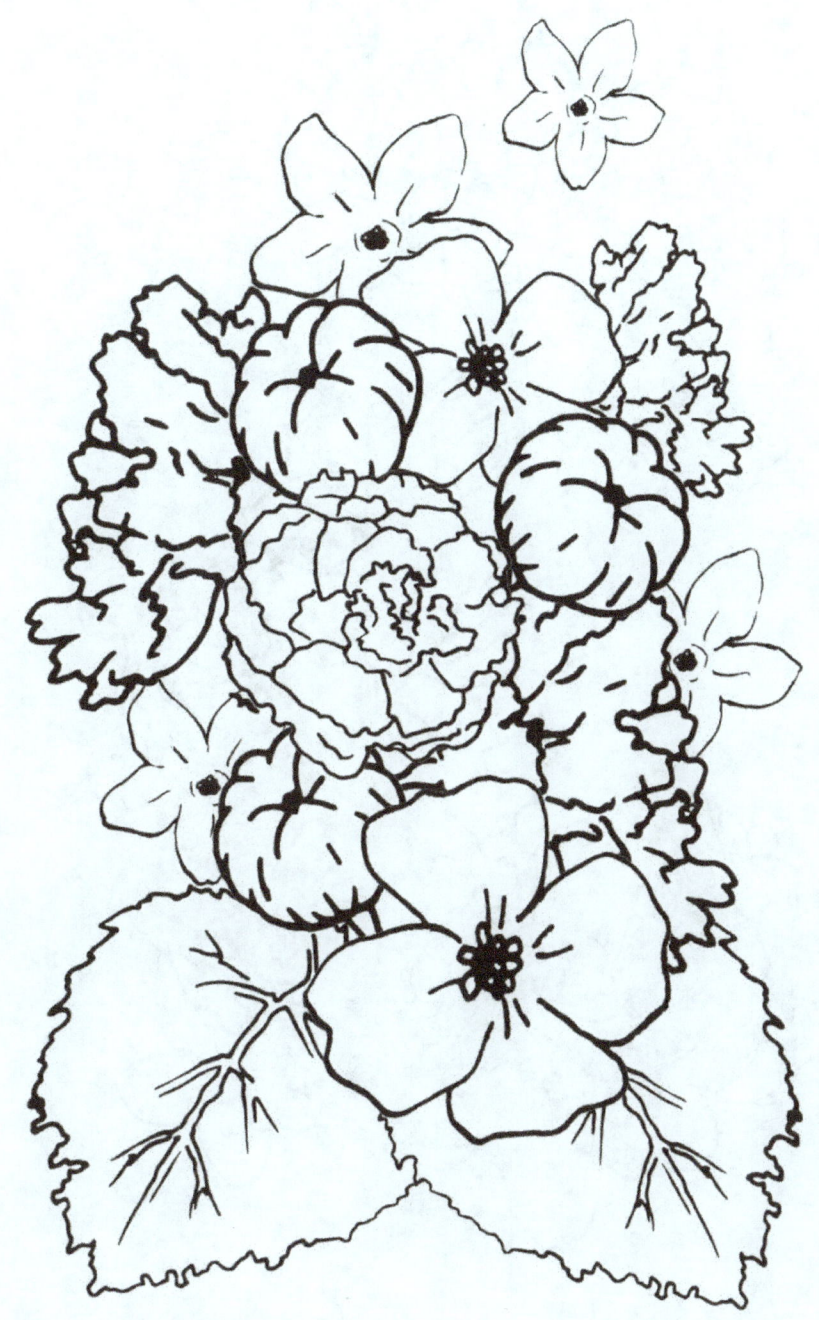

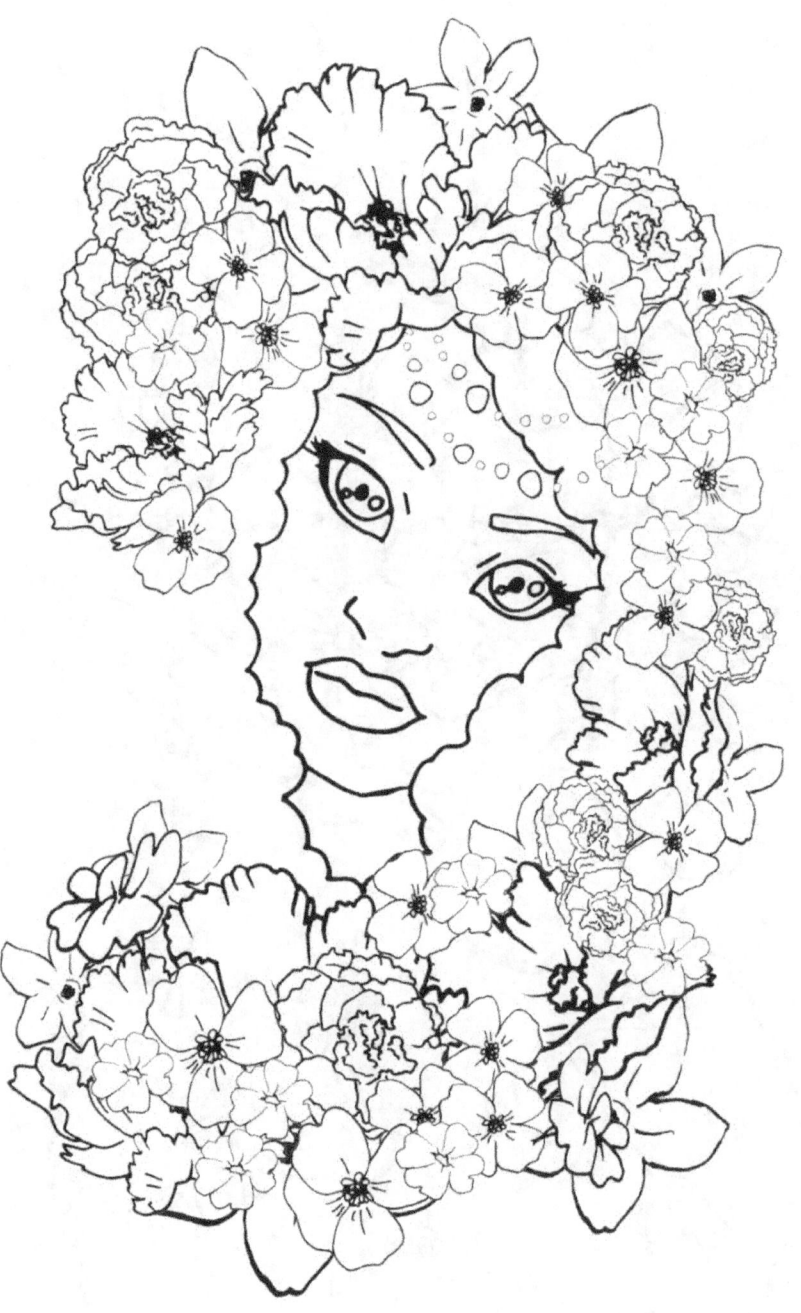

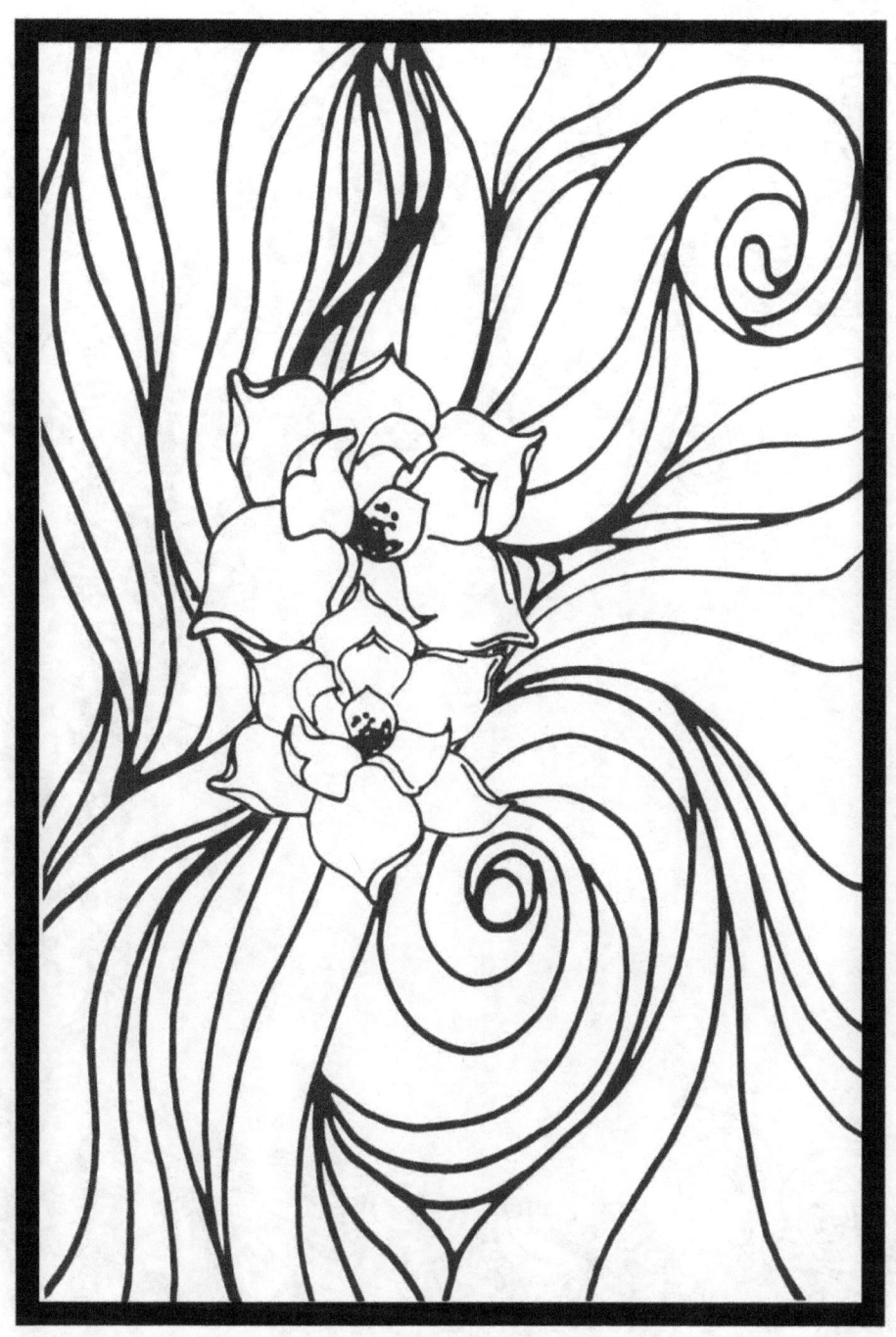

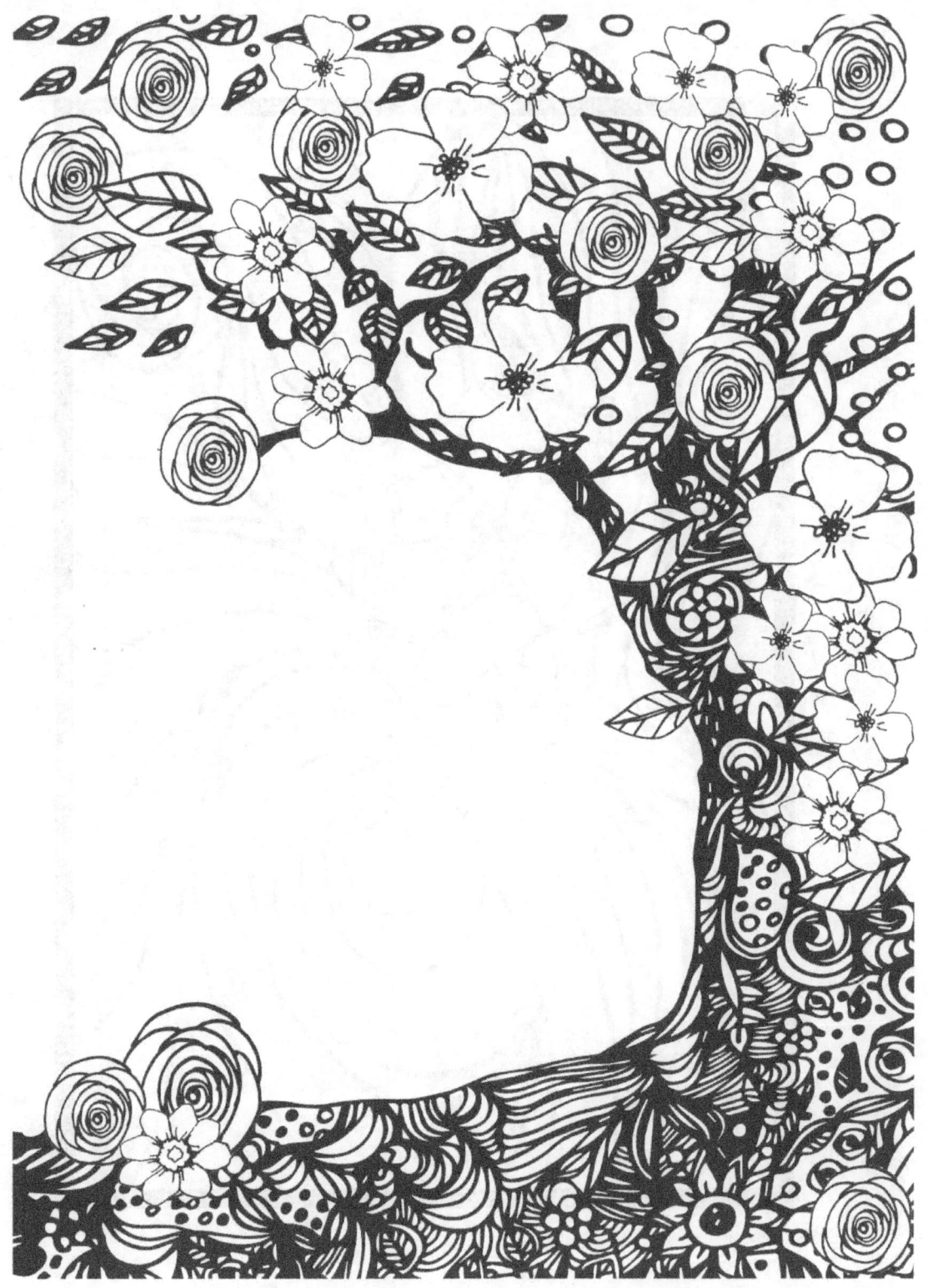

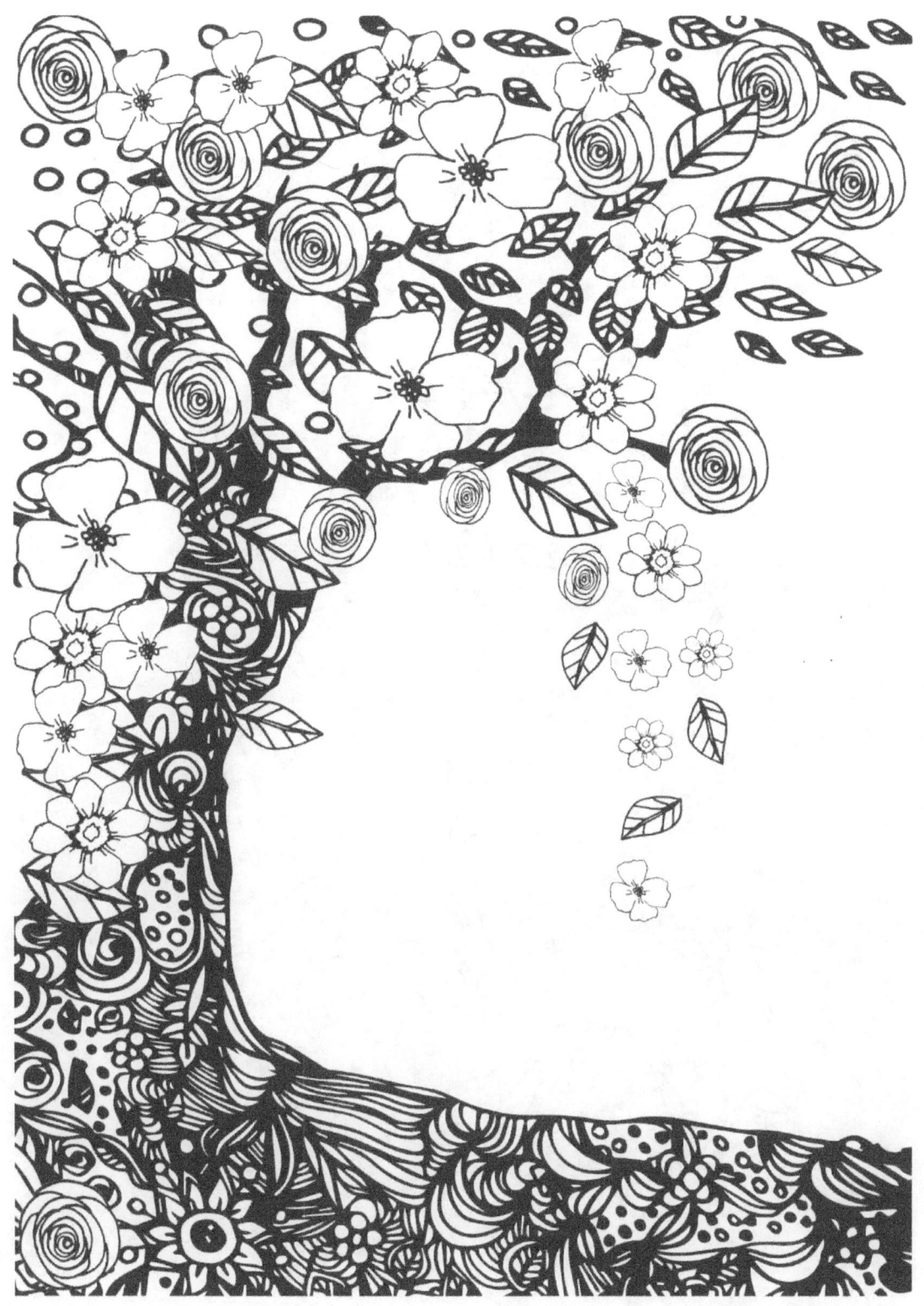

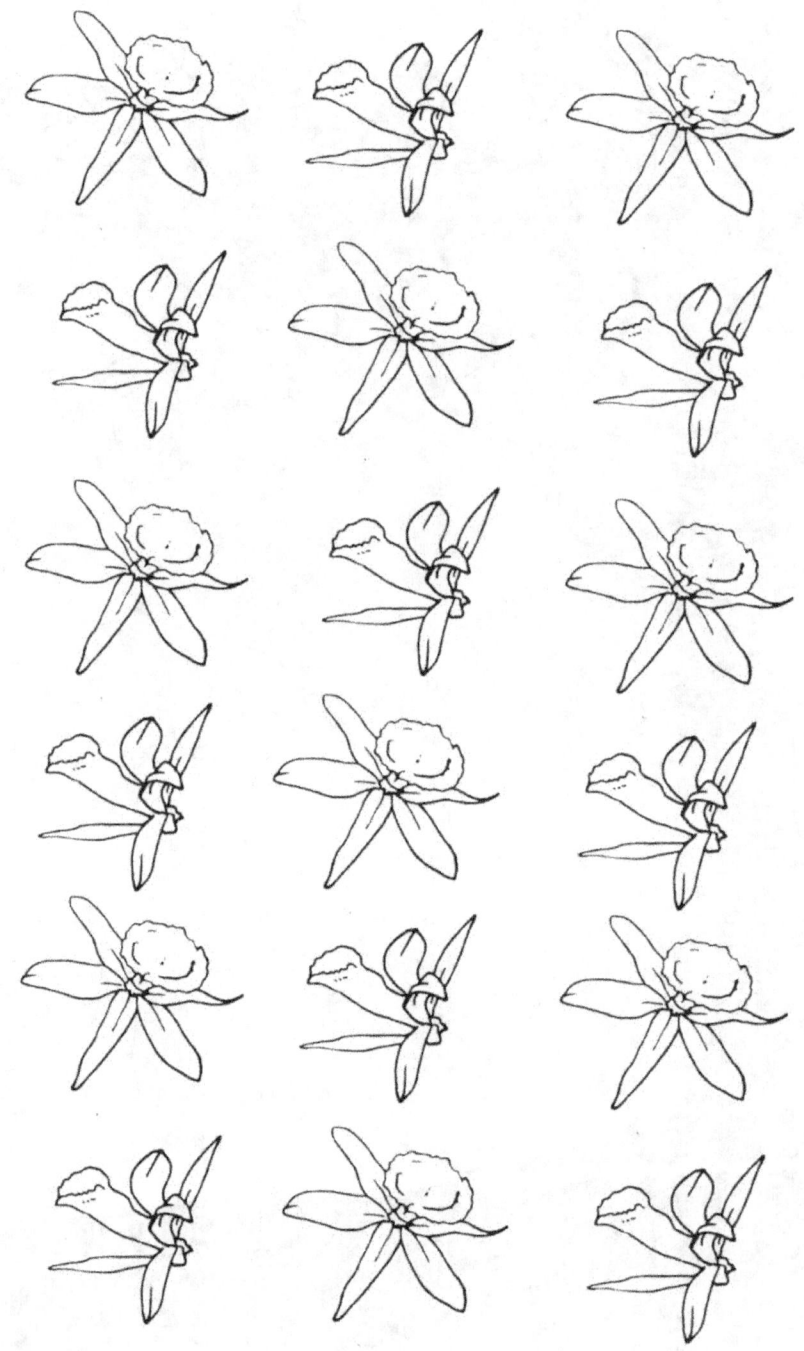

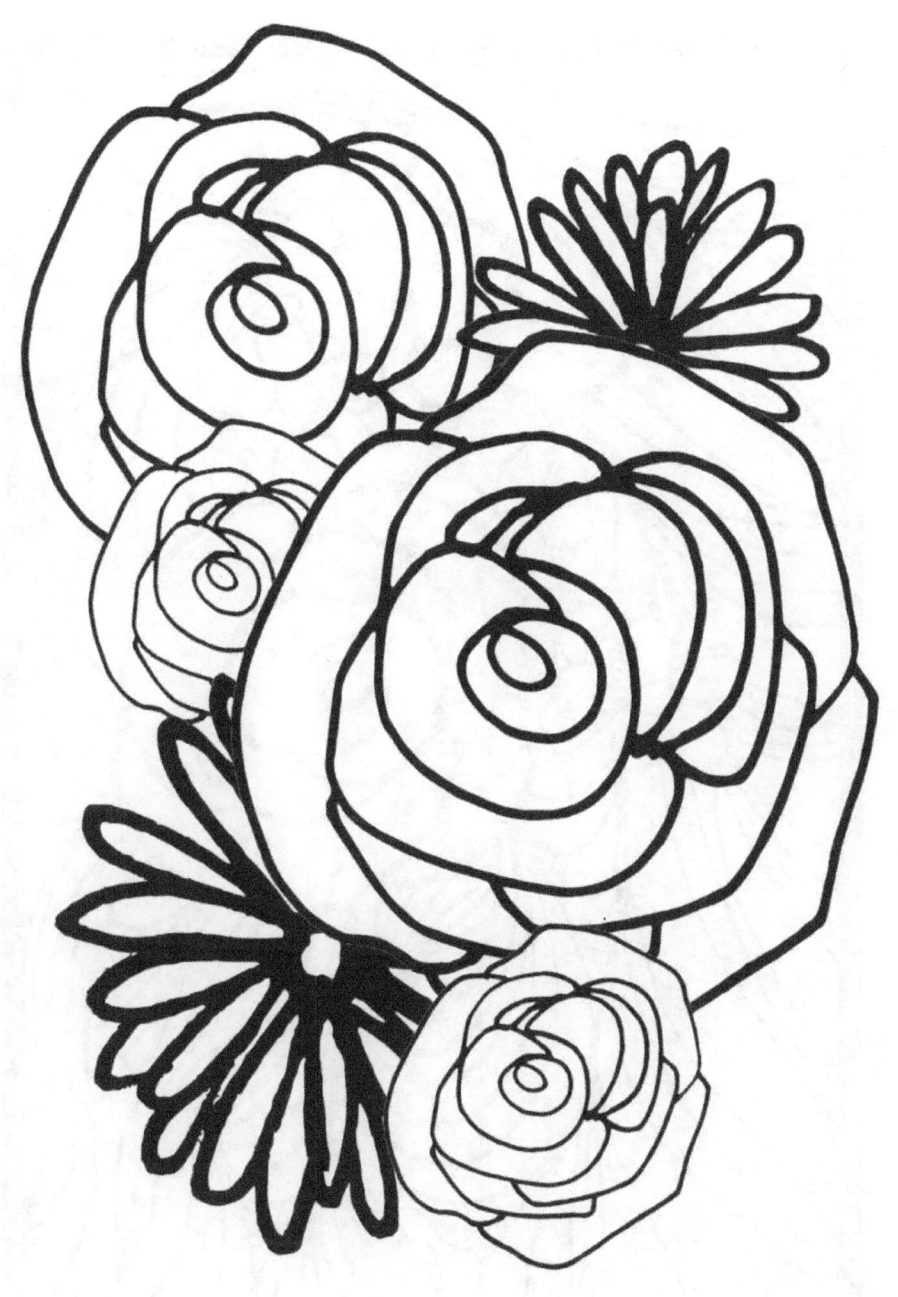

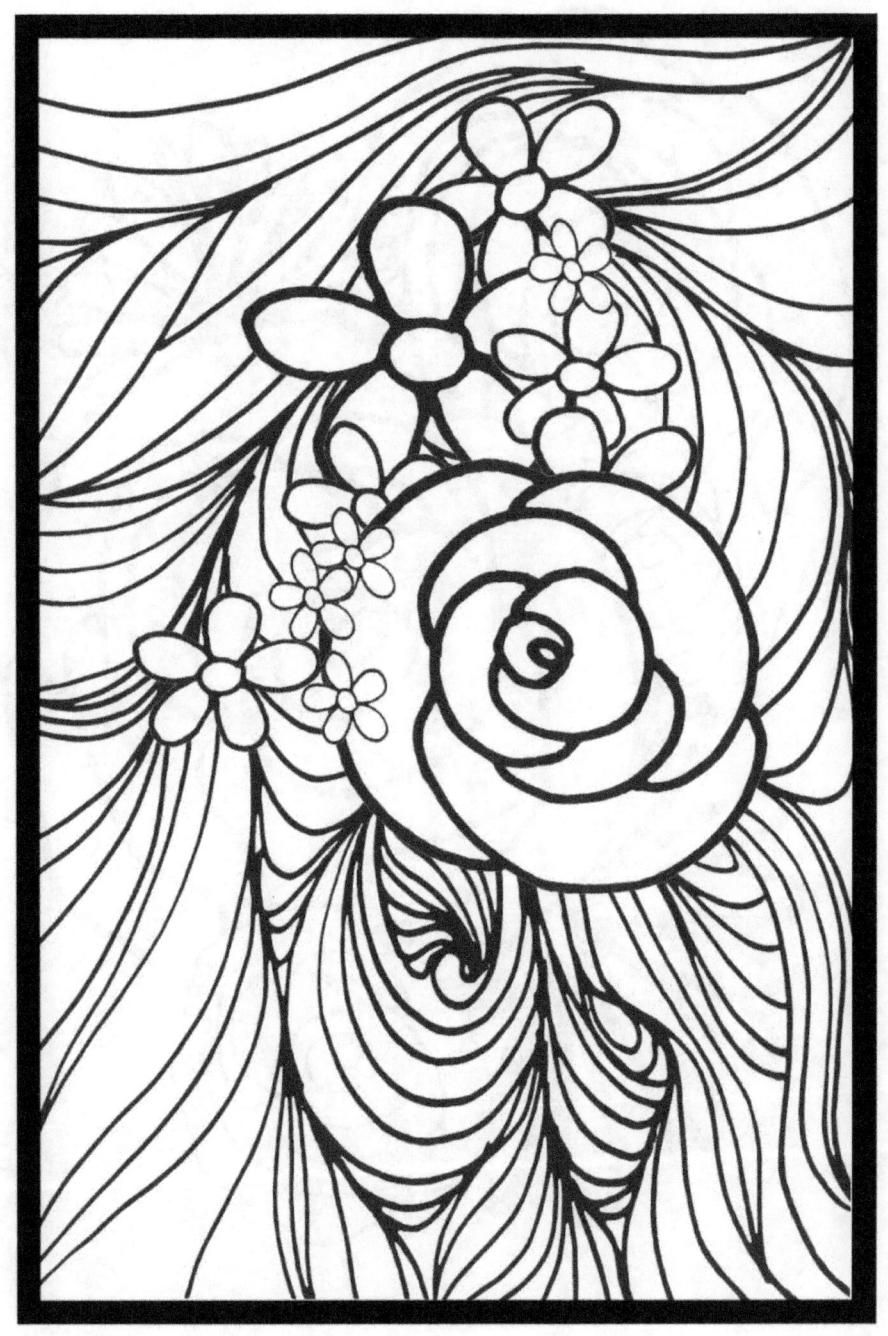

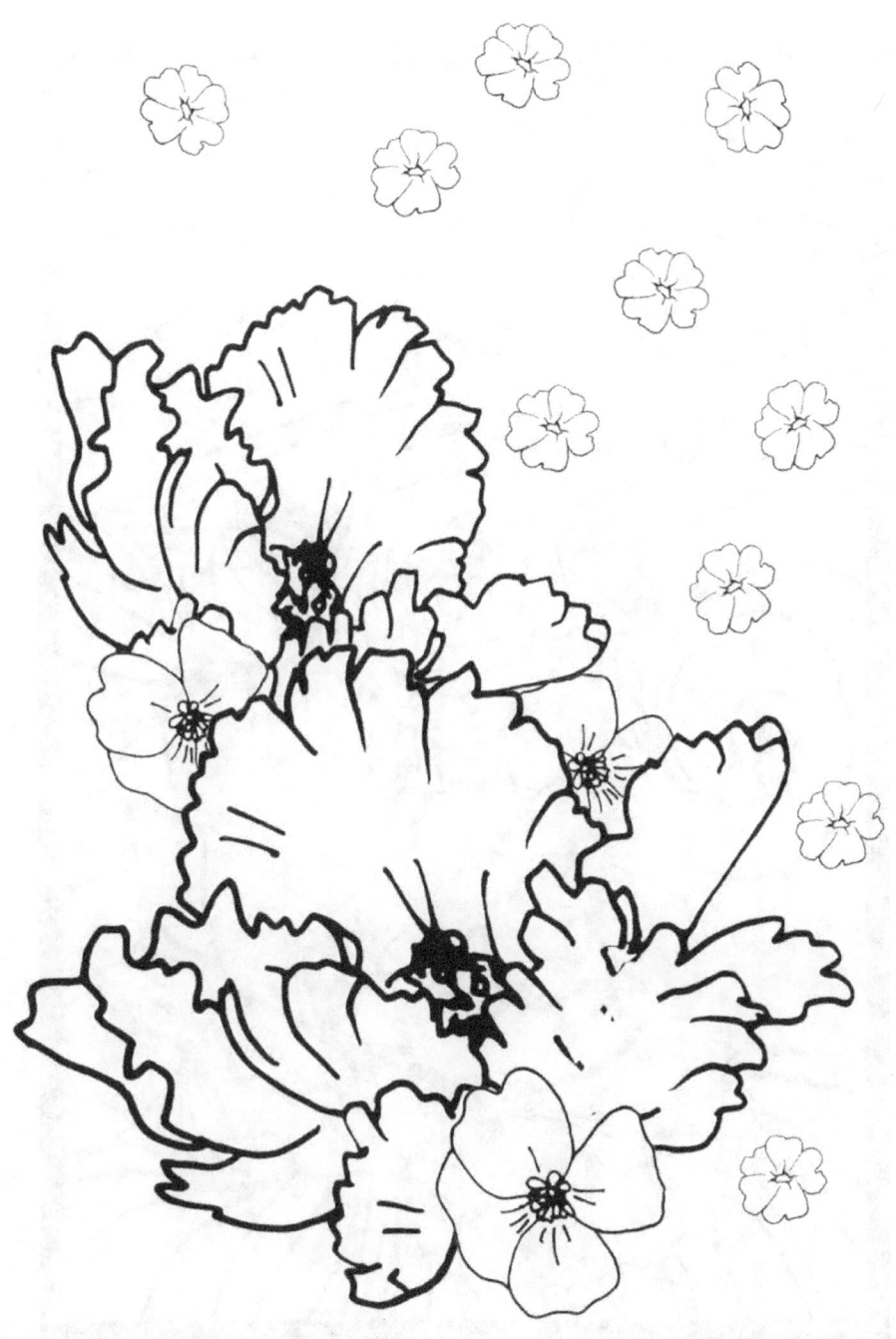

17

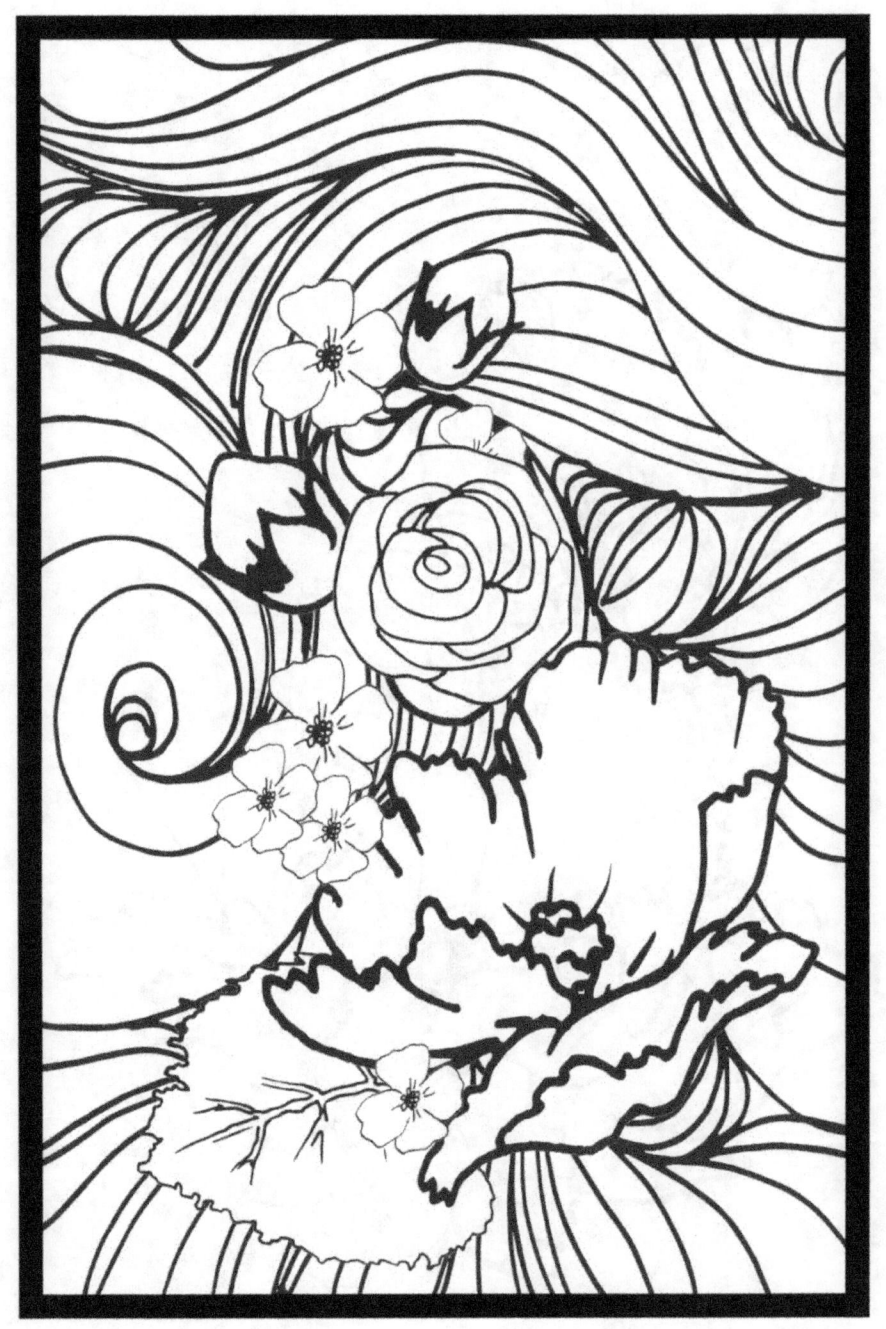

18

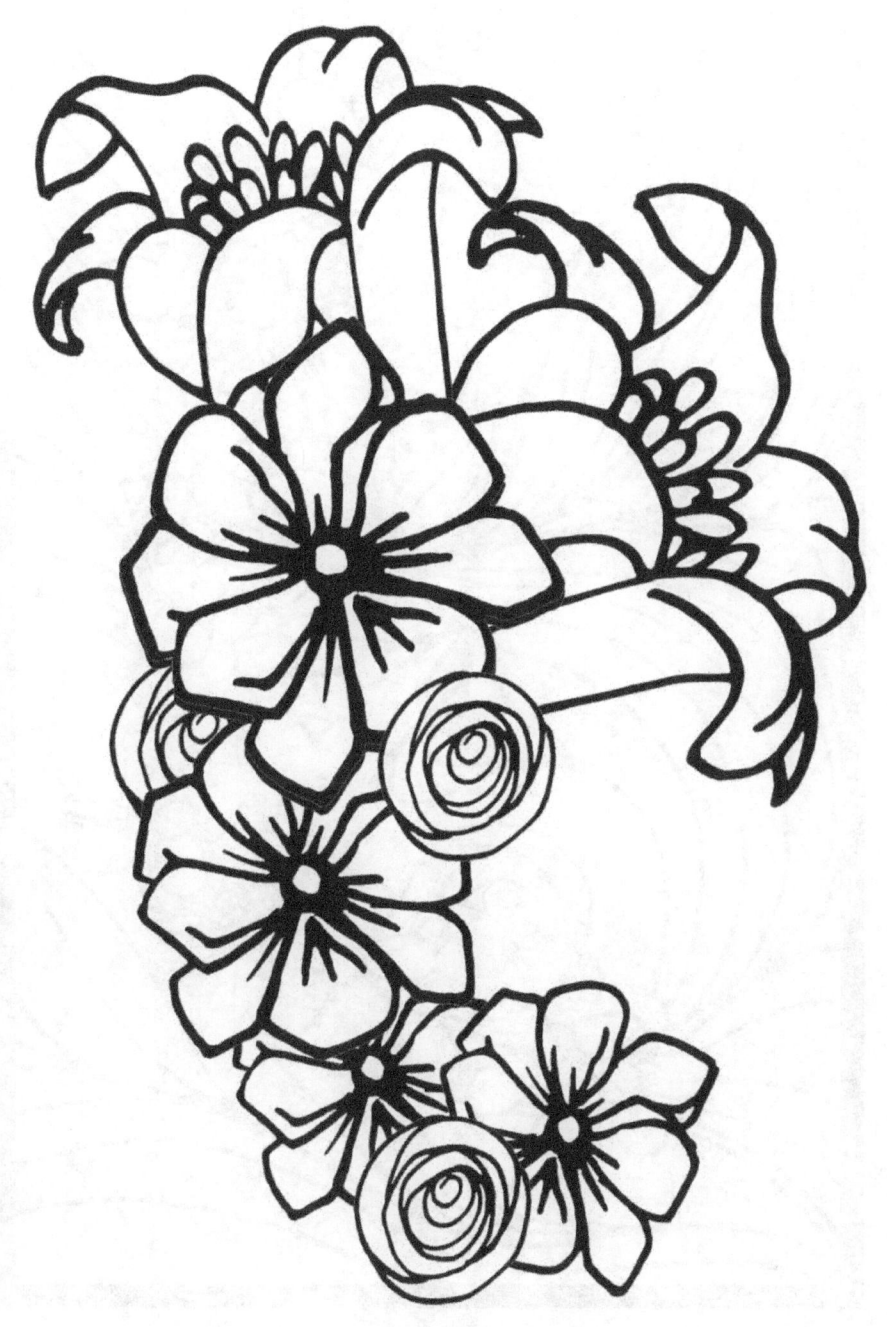

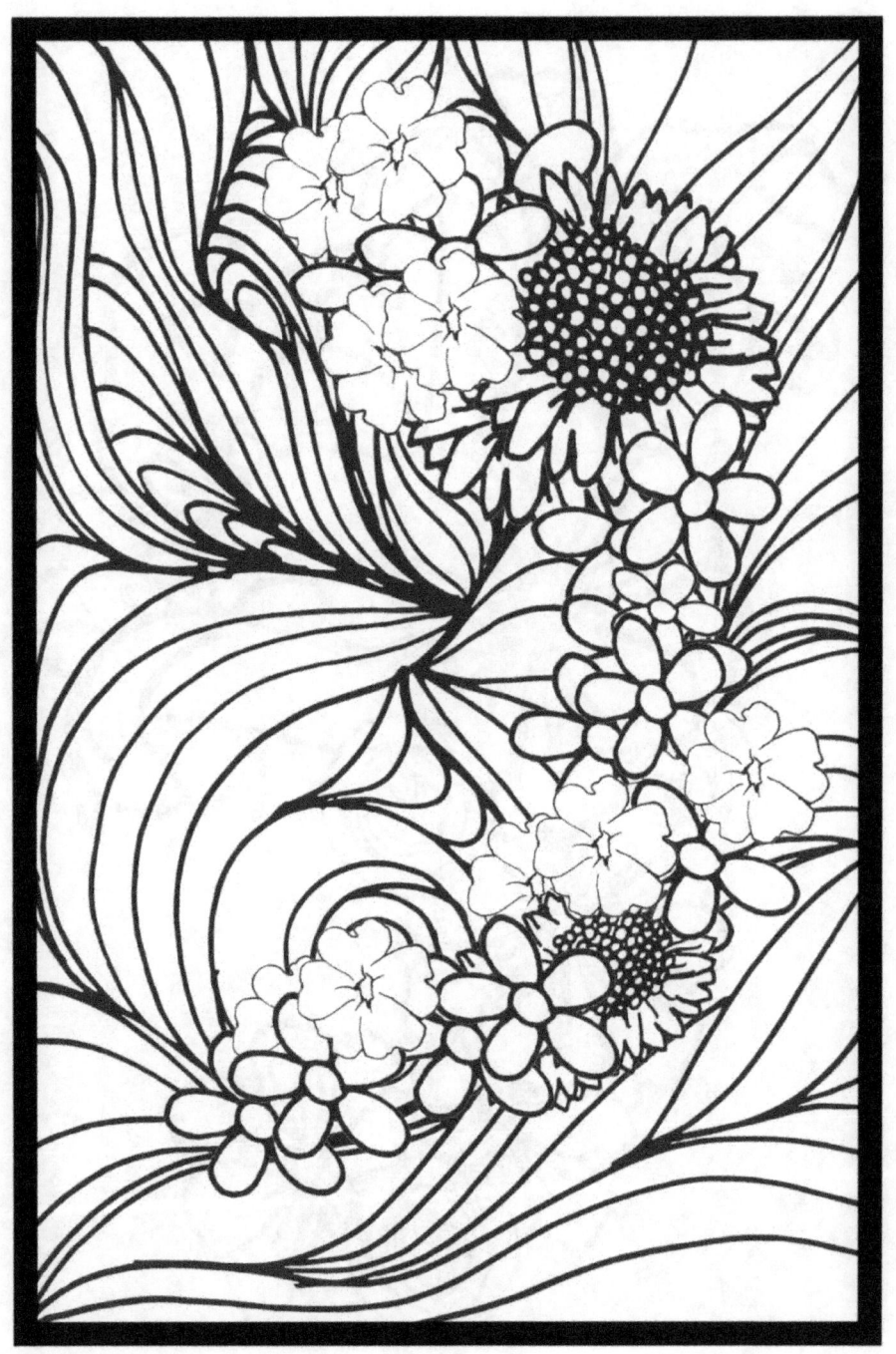

20

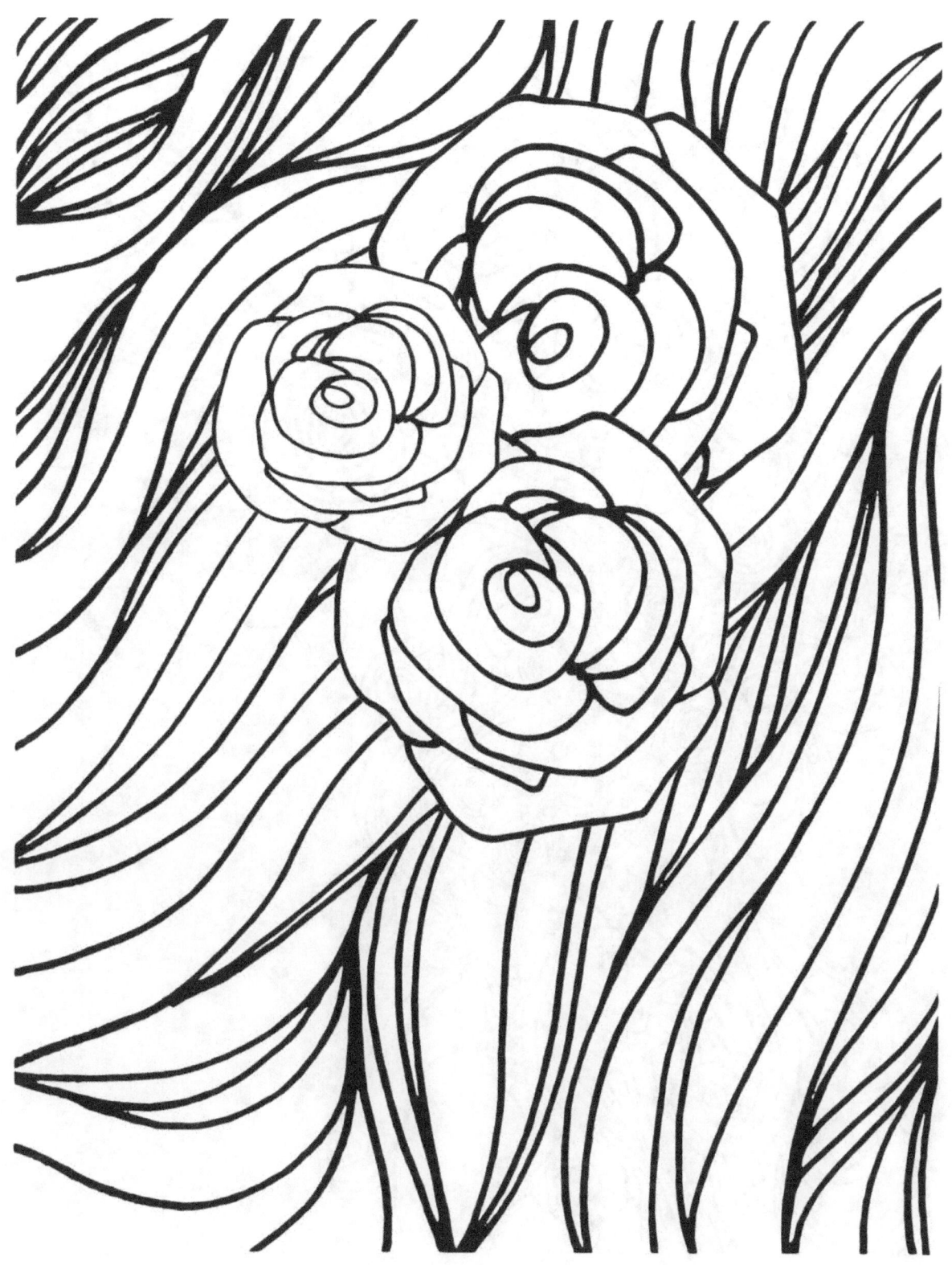

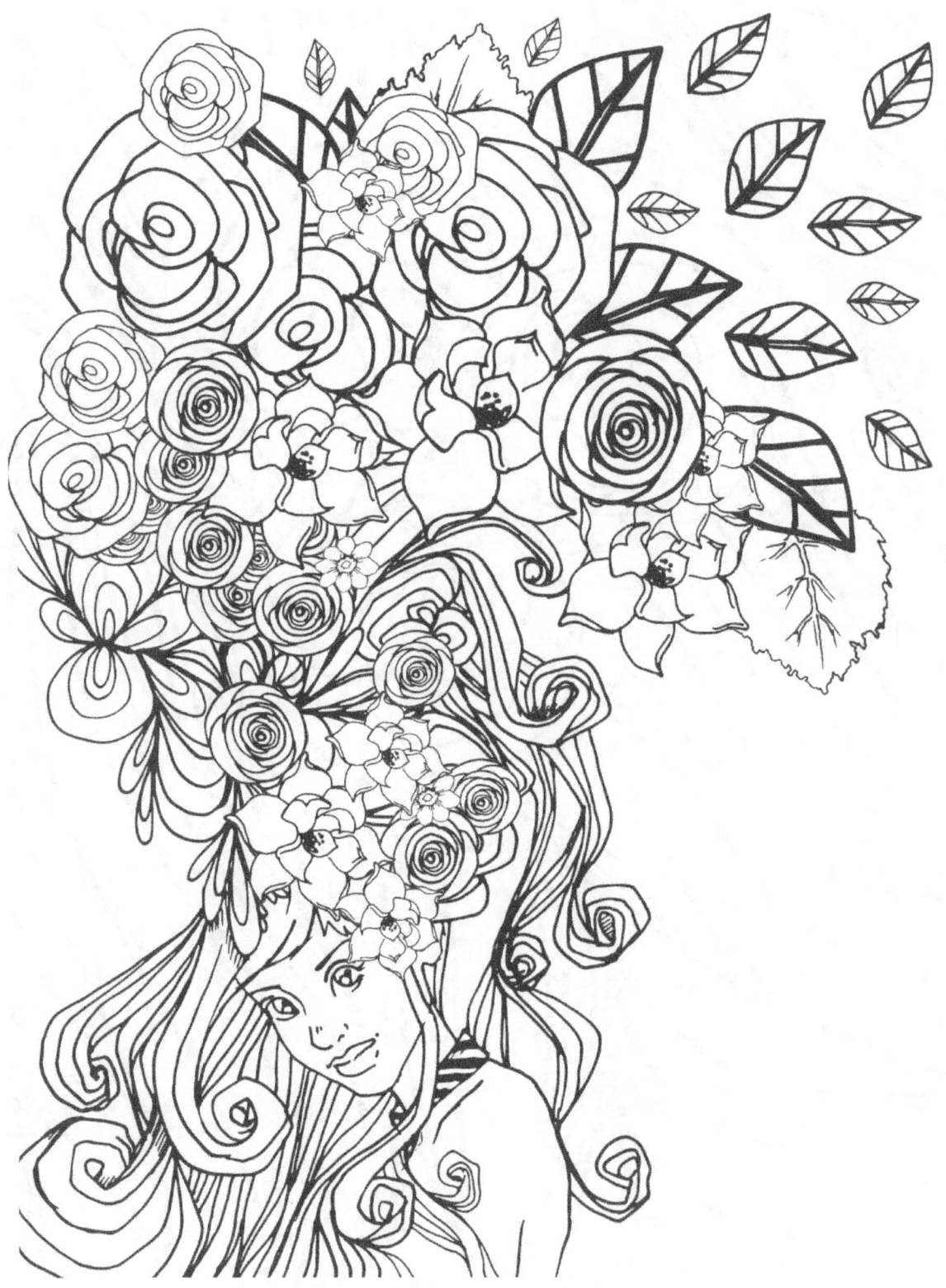

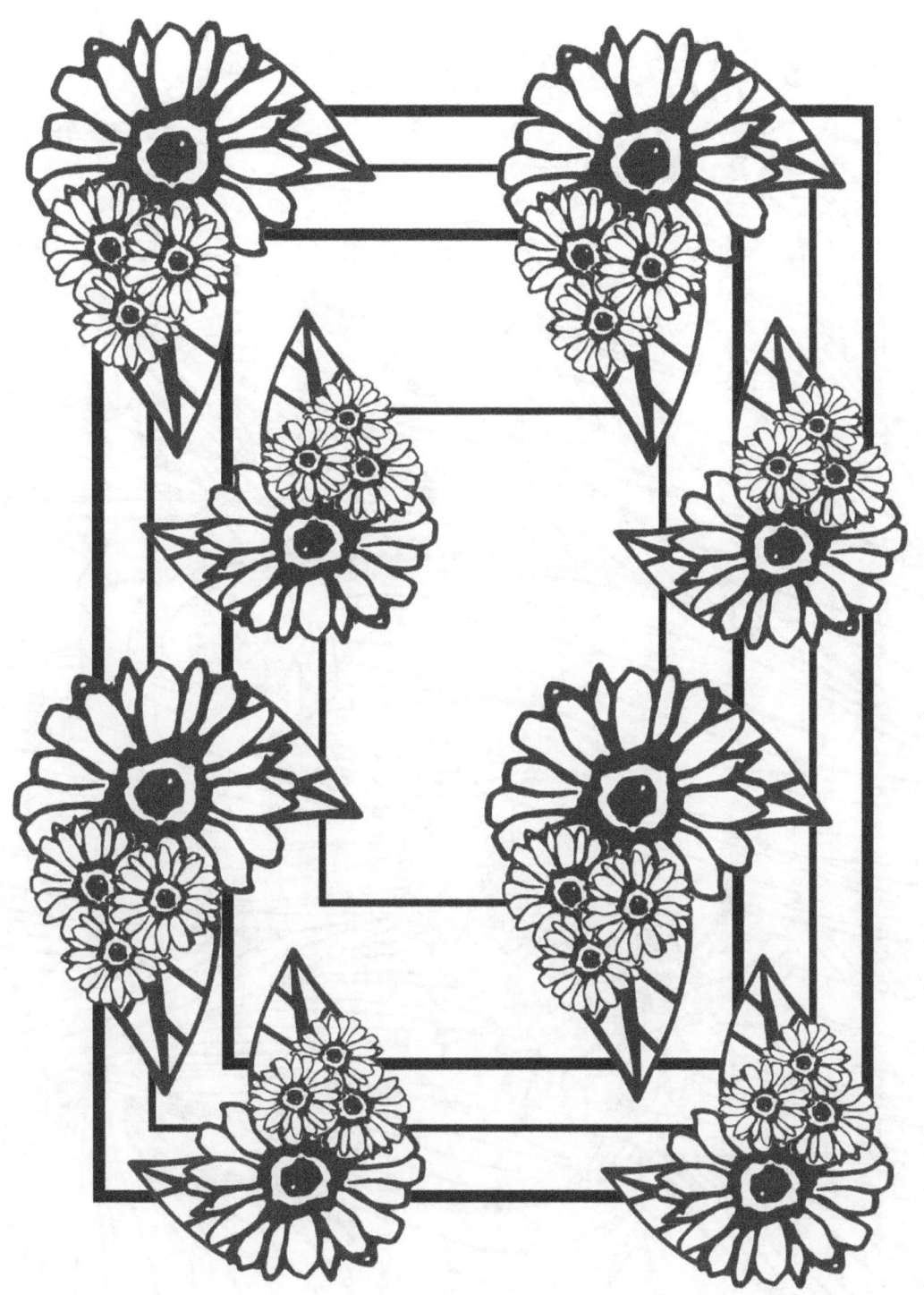

23

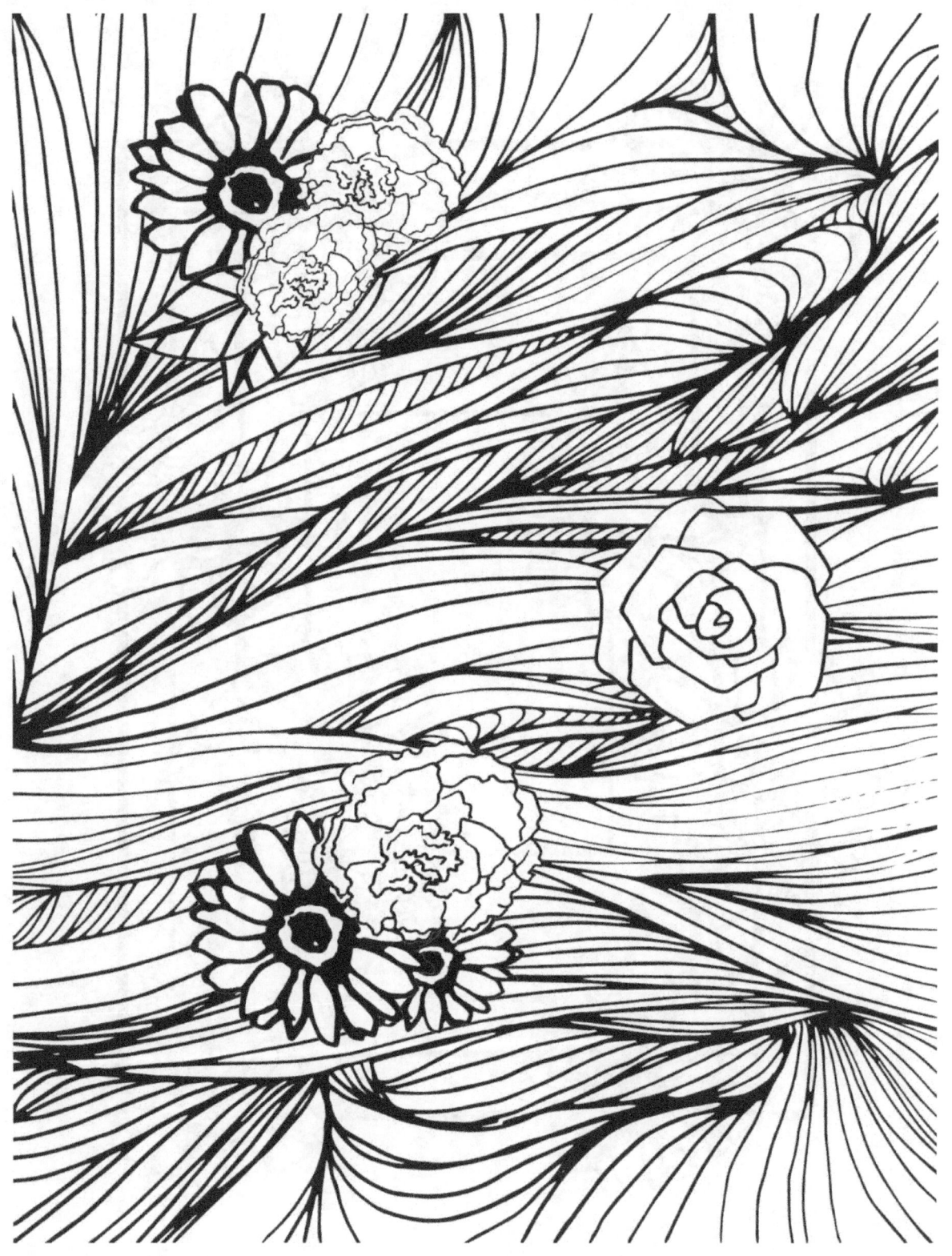

24

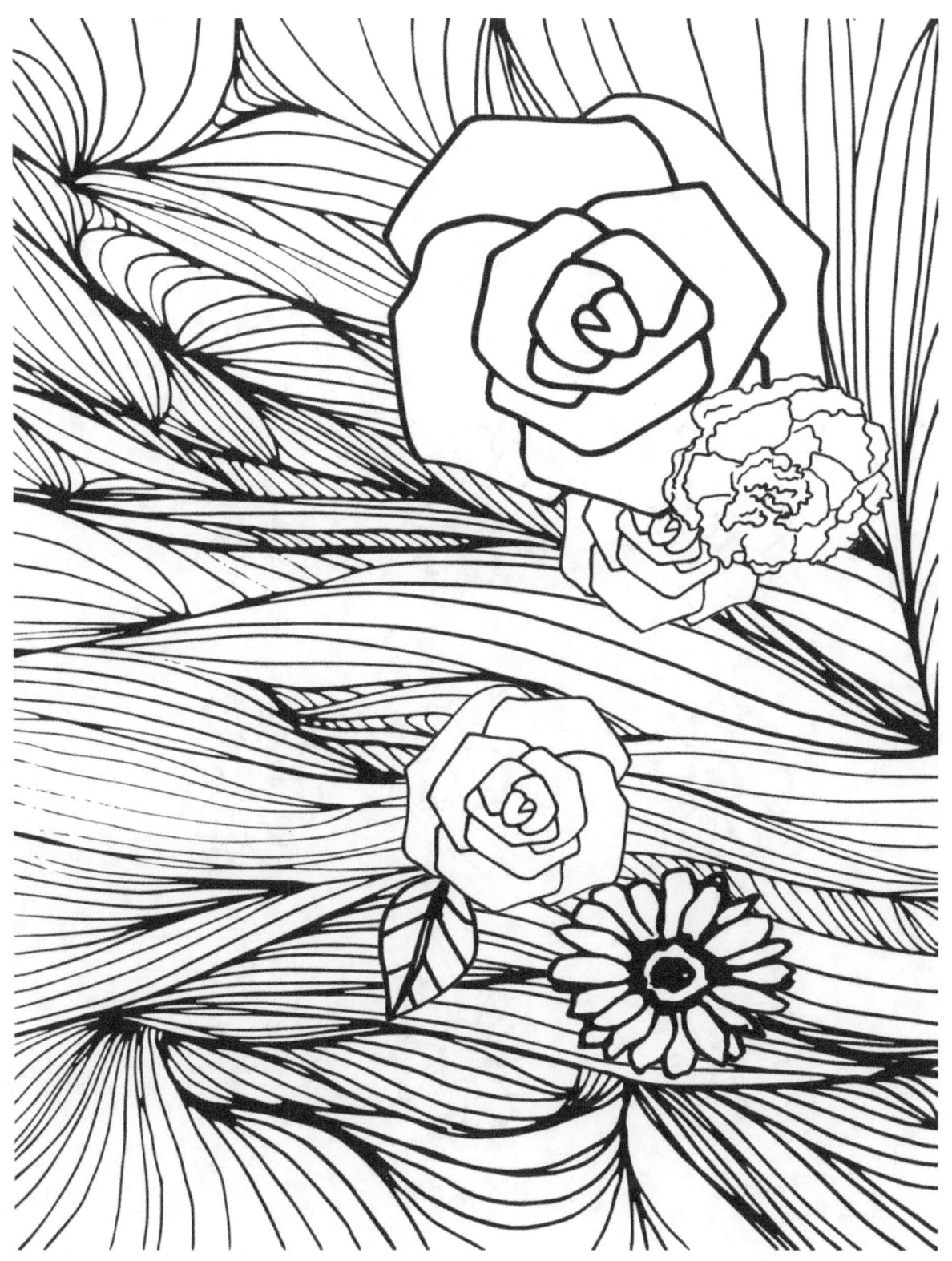

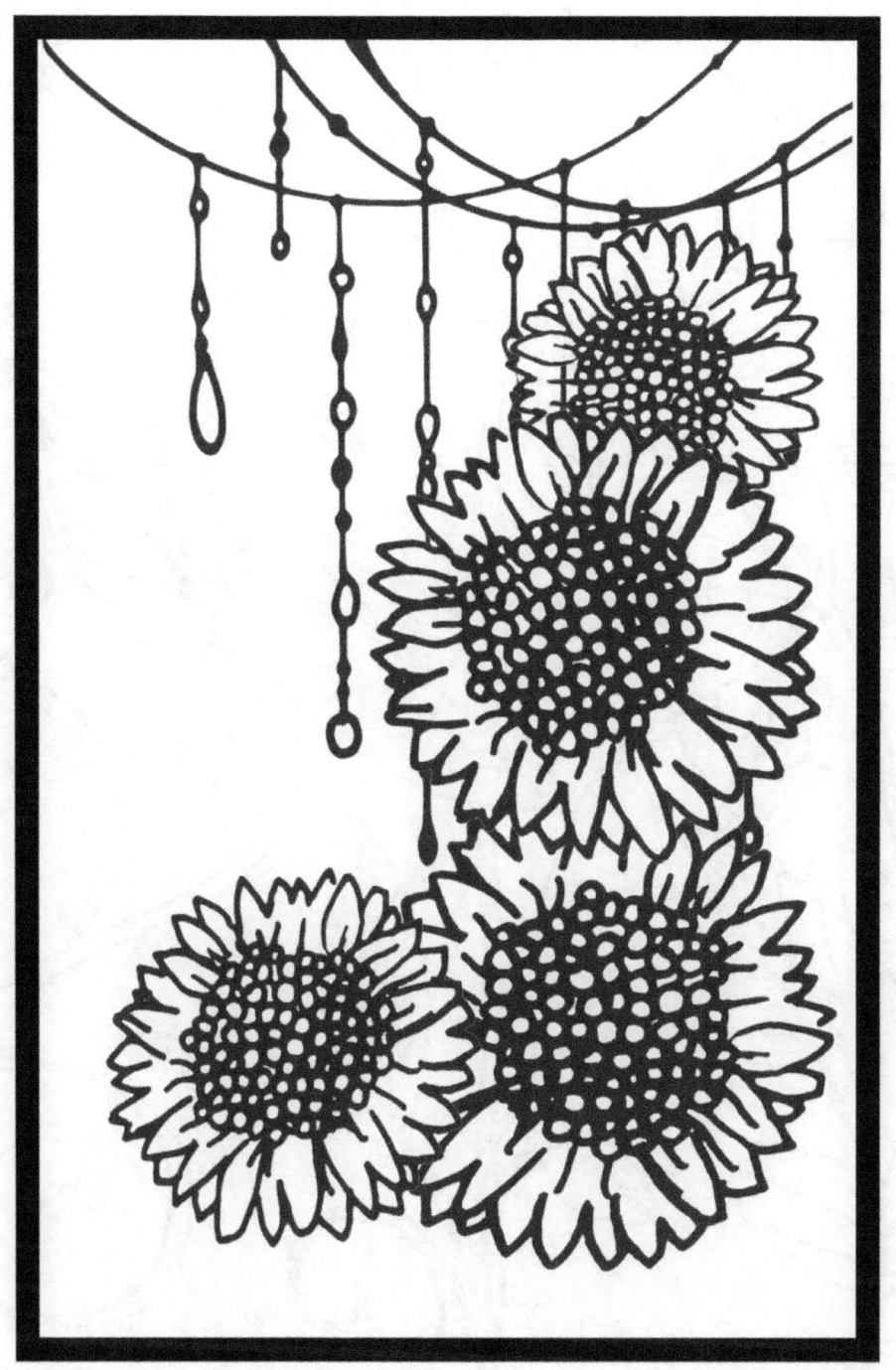

28

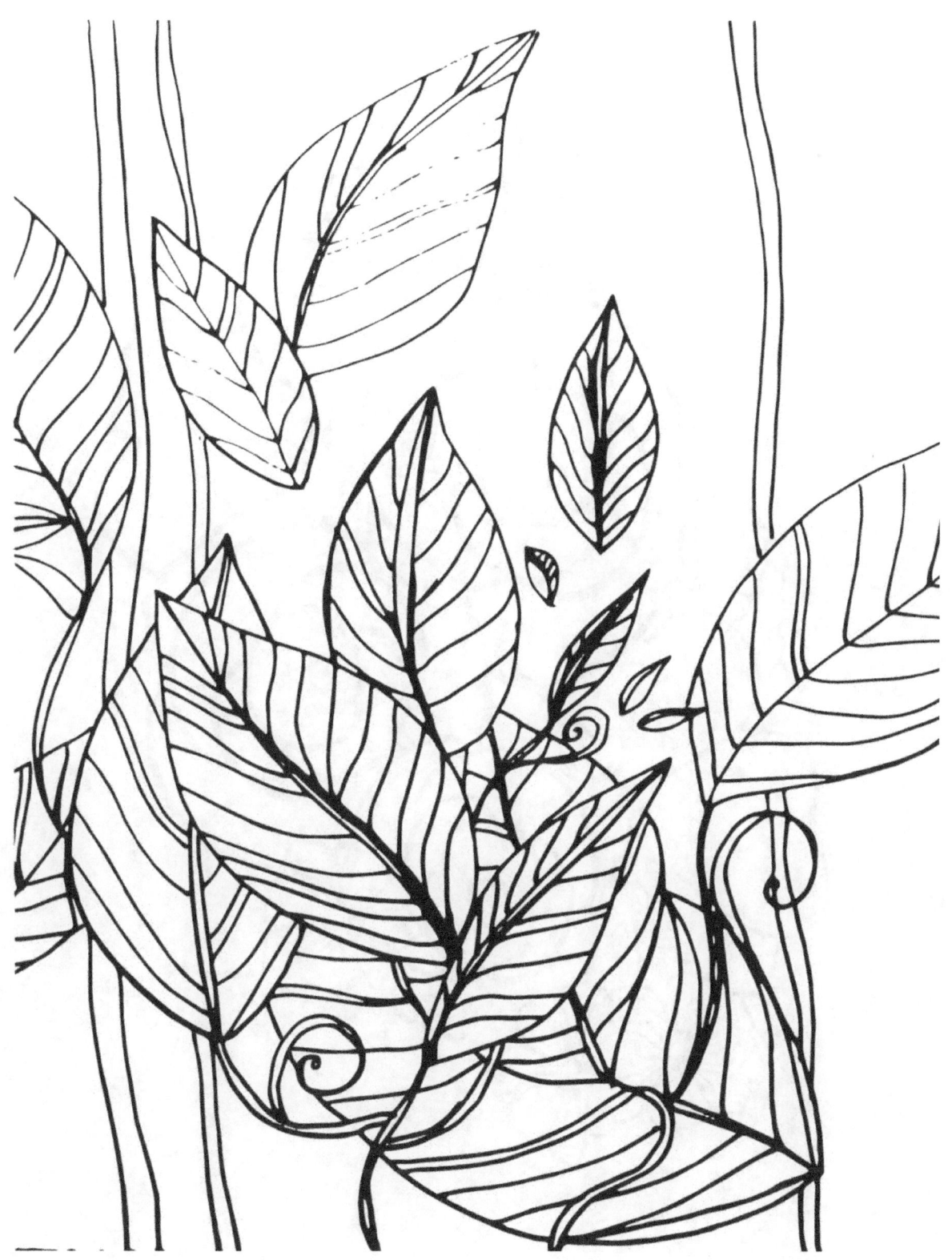

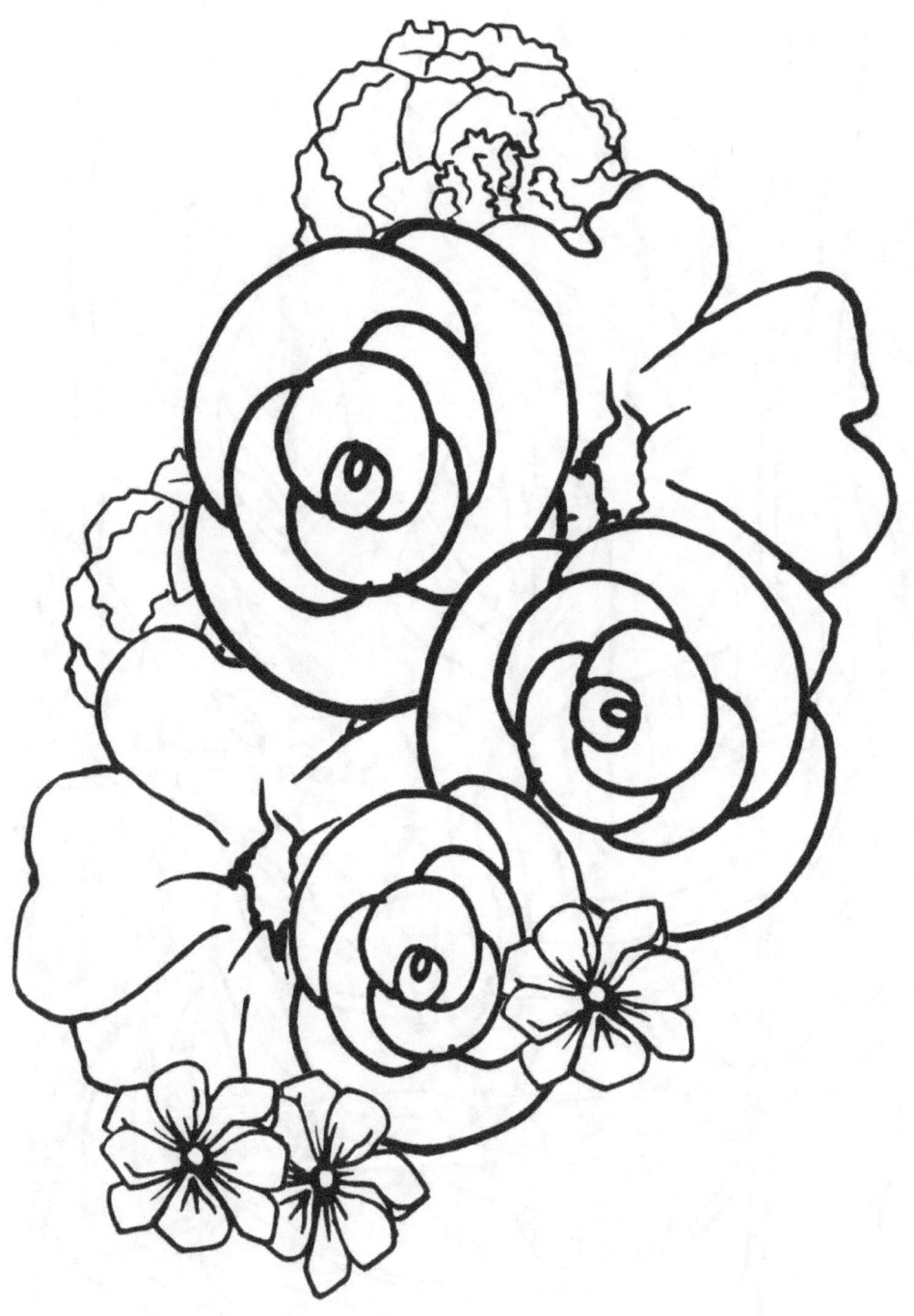

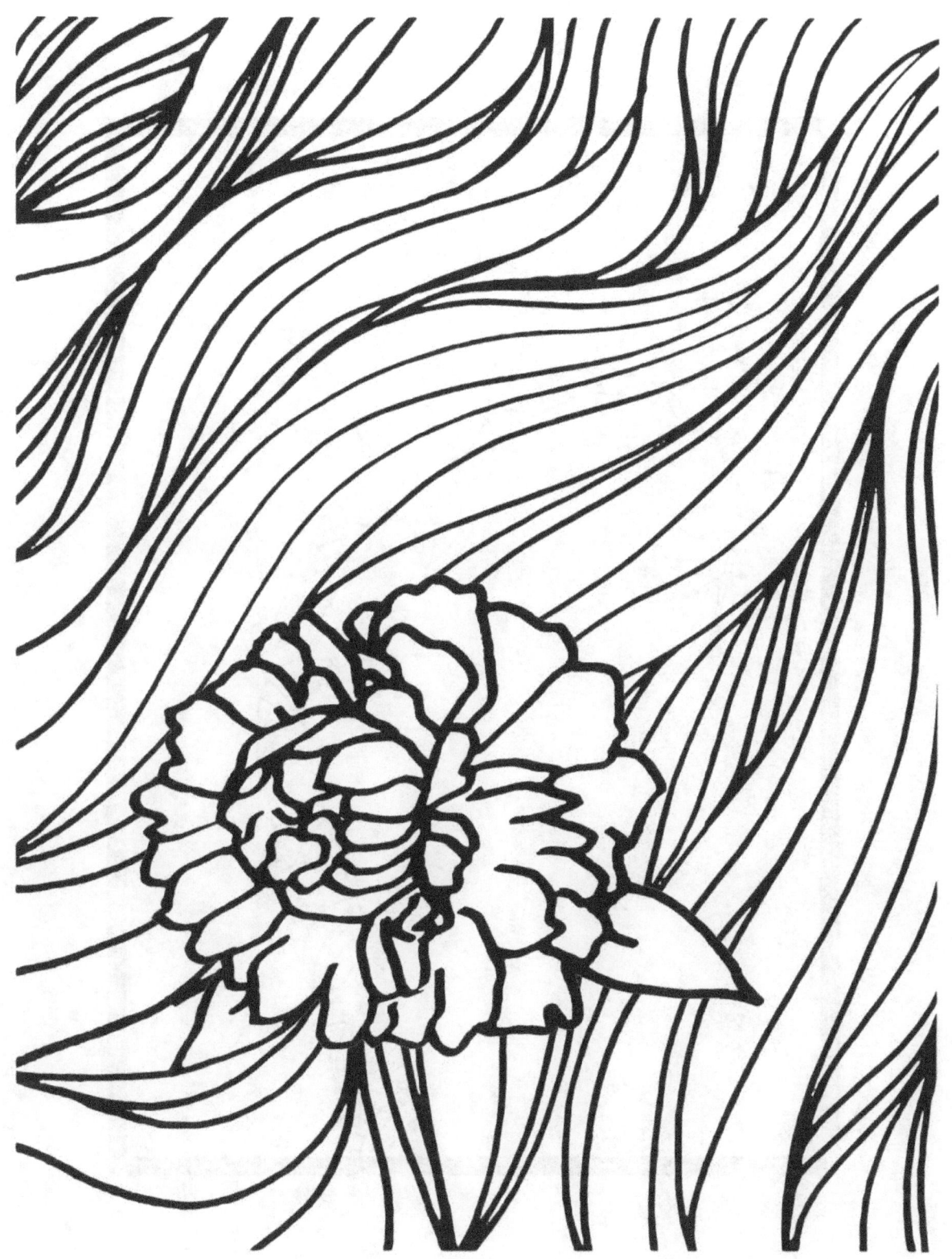

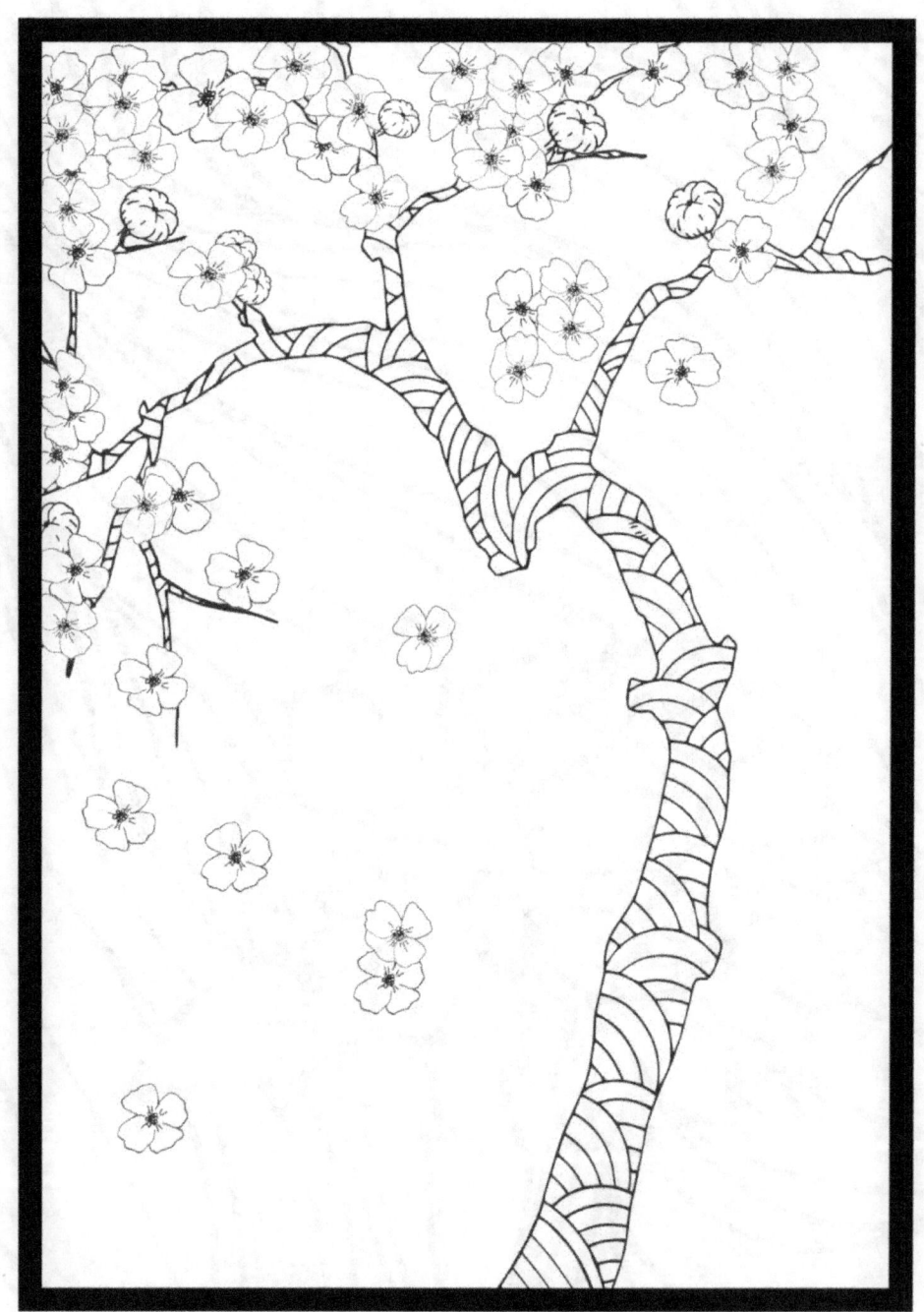

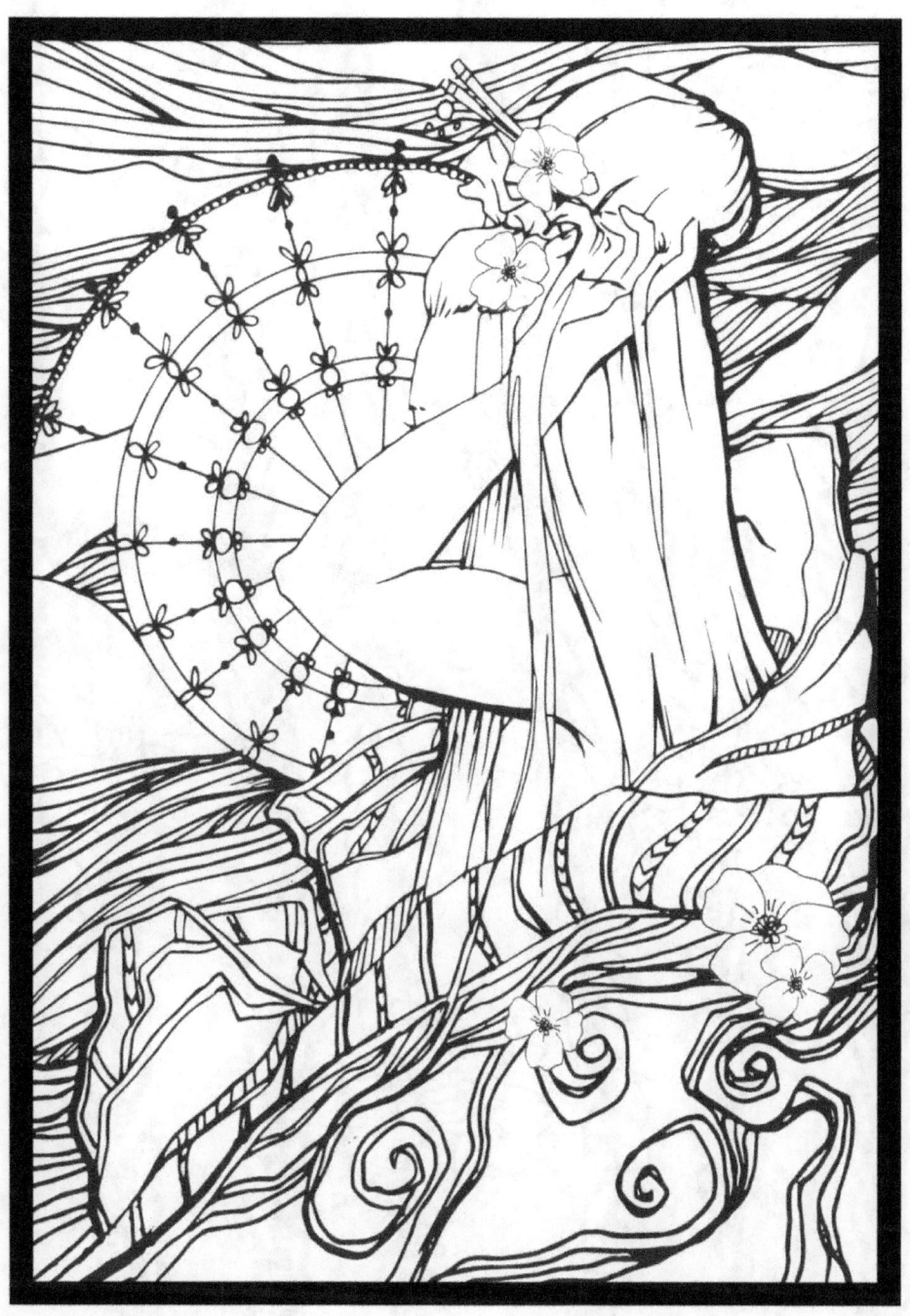

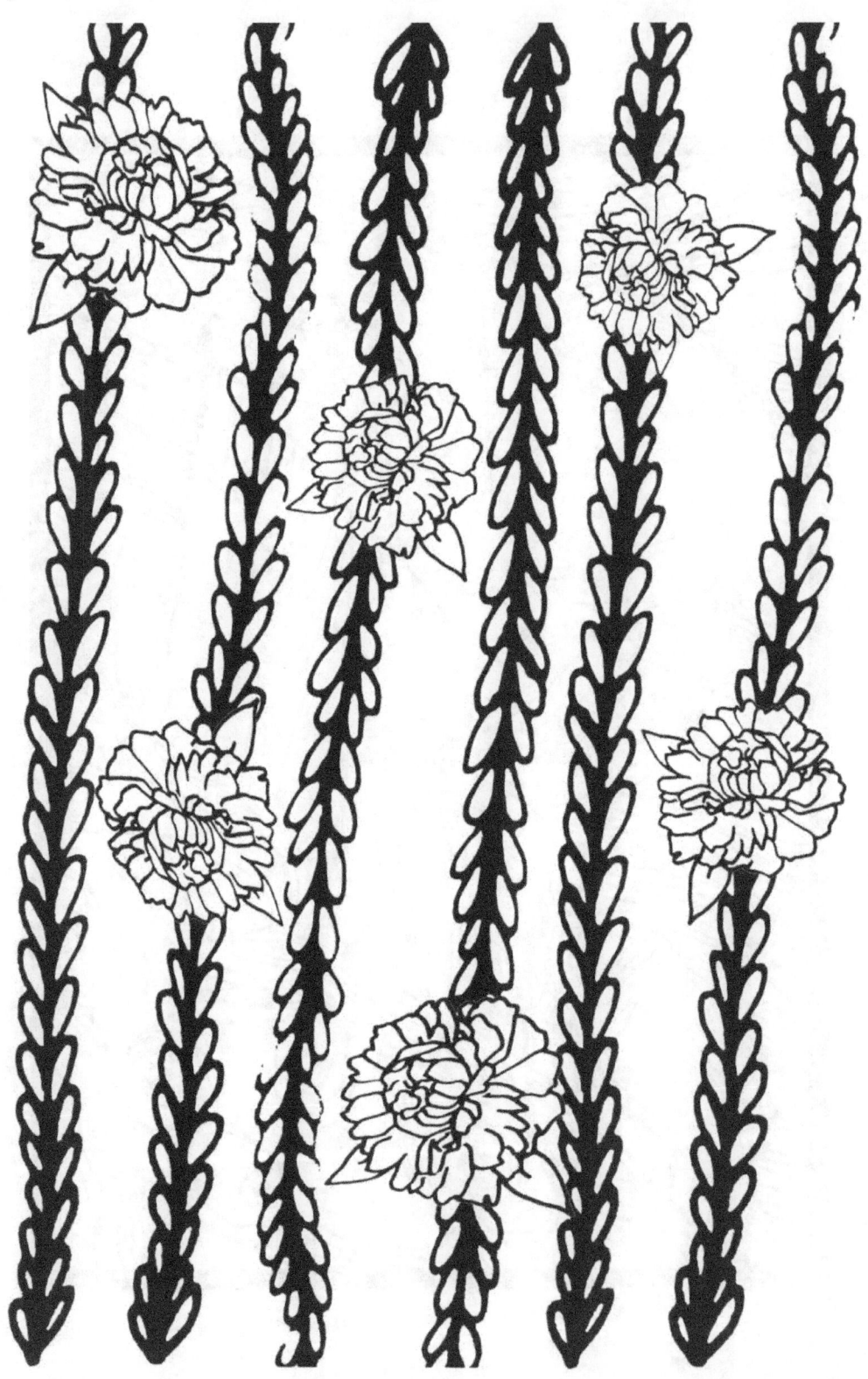

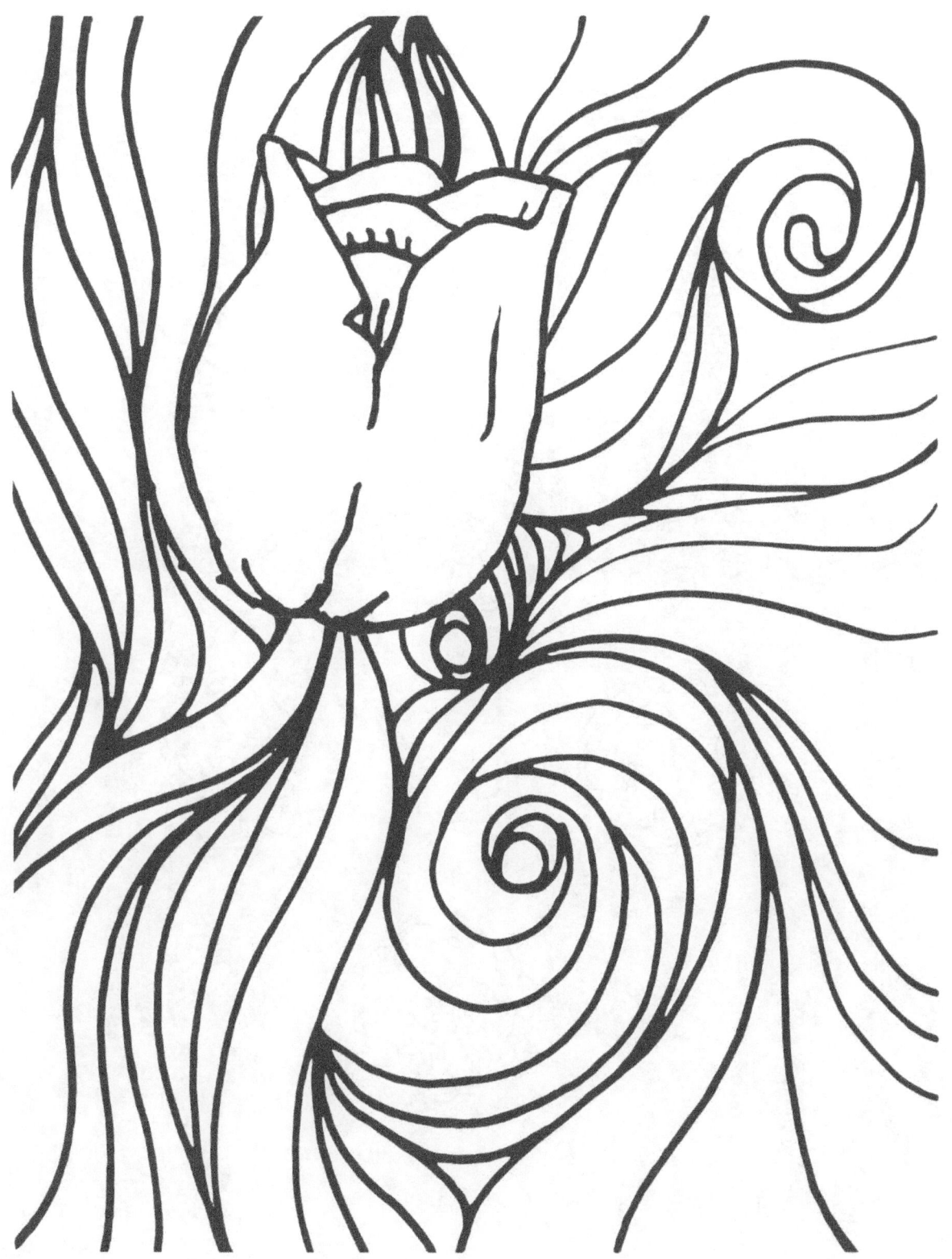

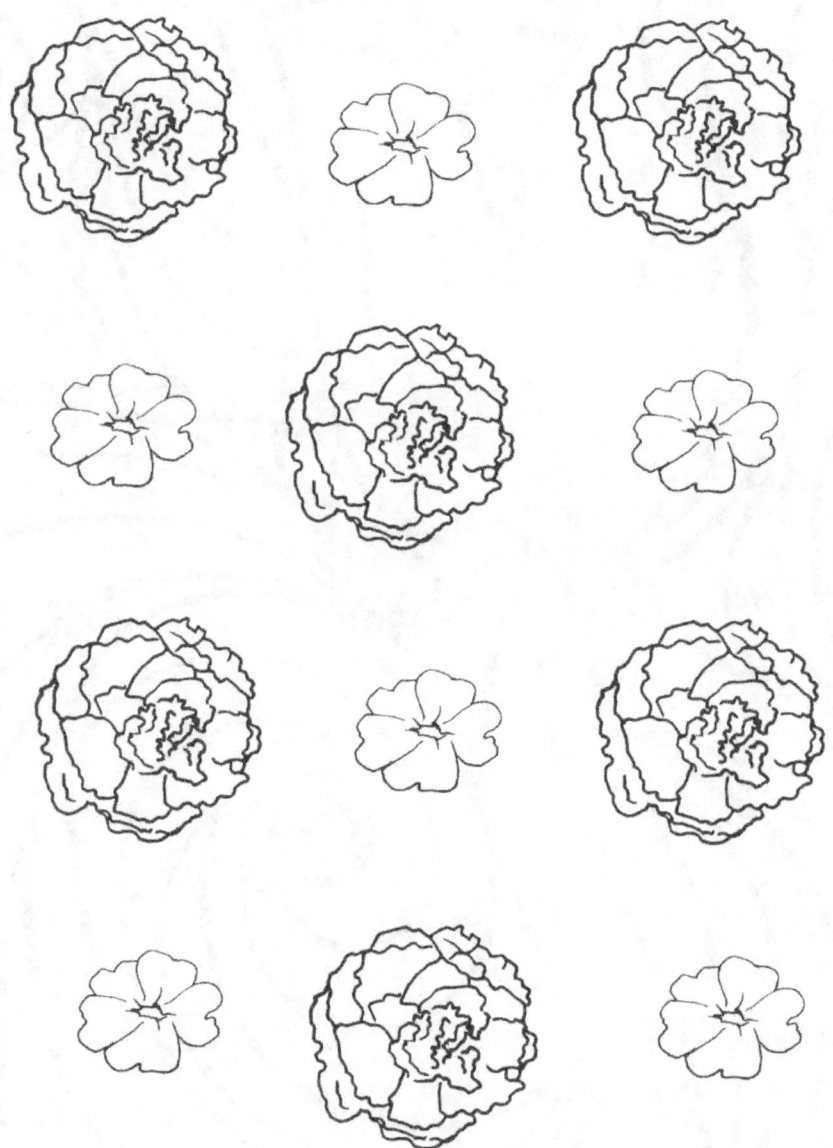

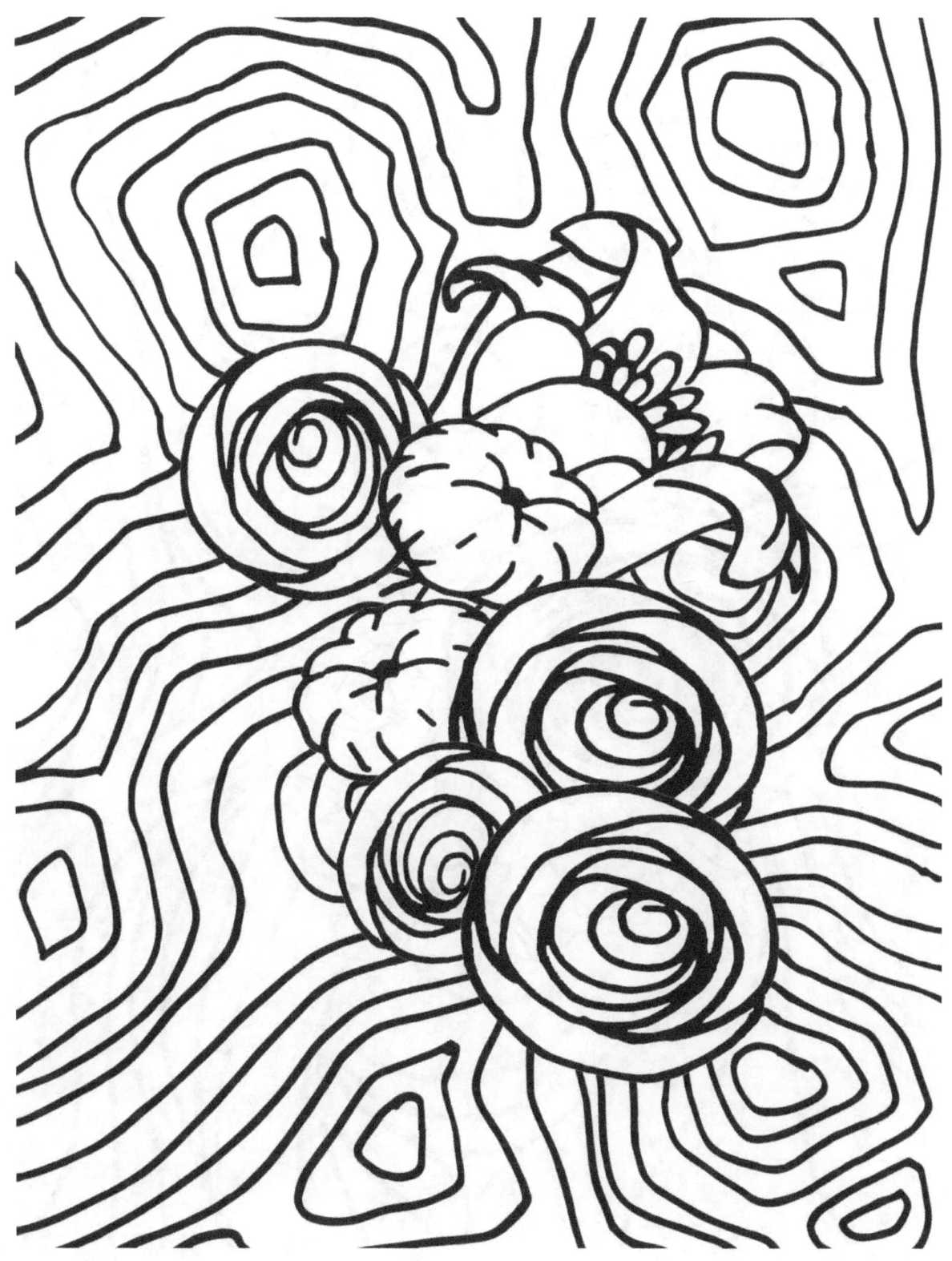

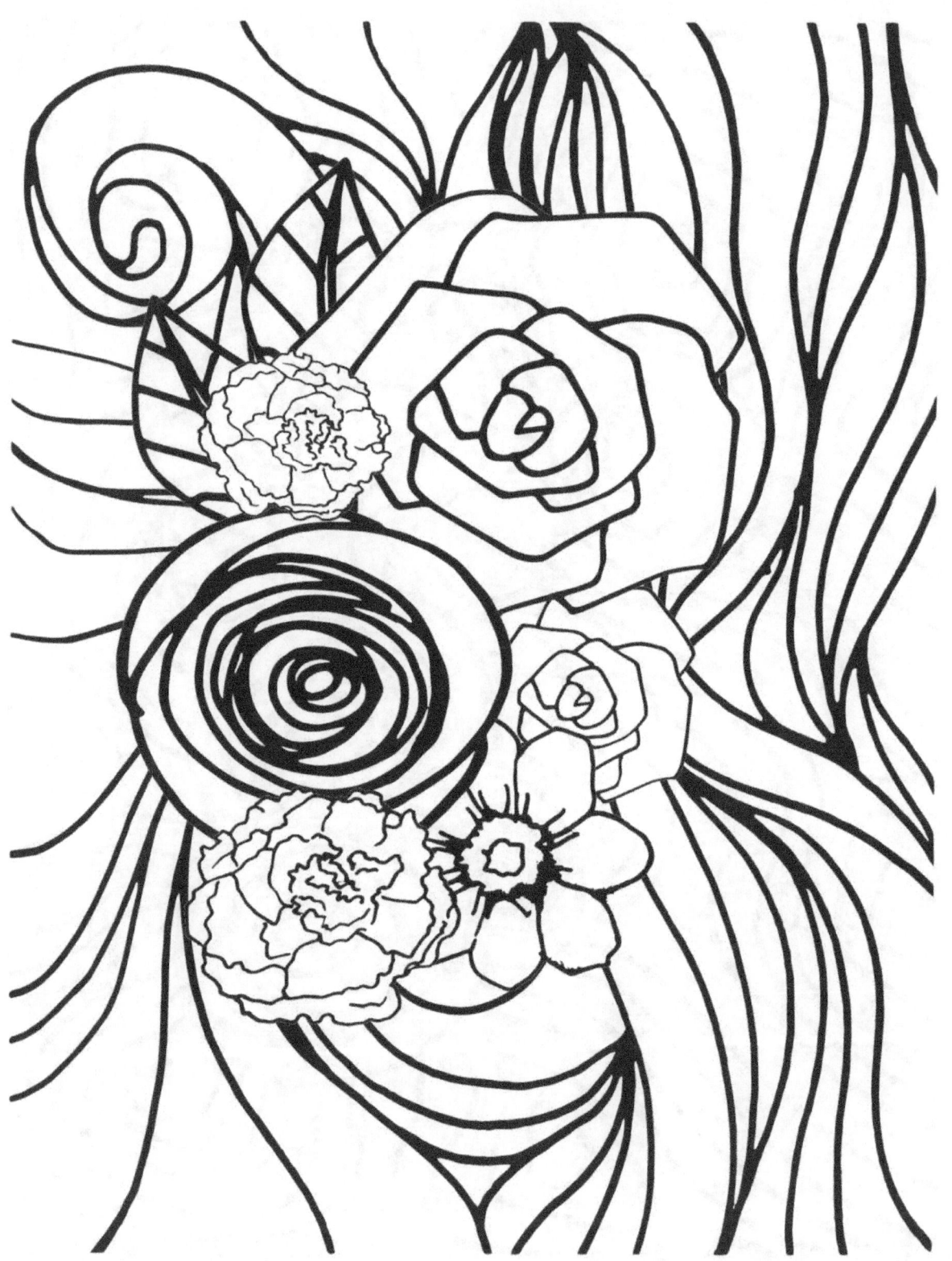

38

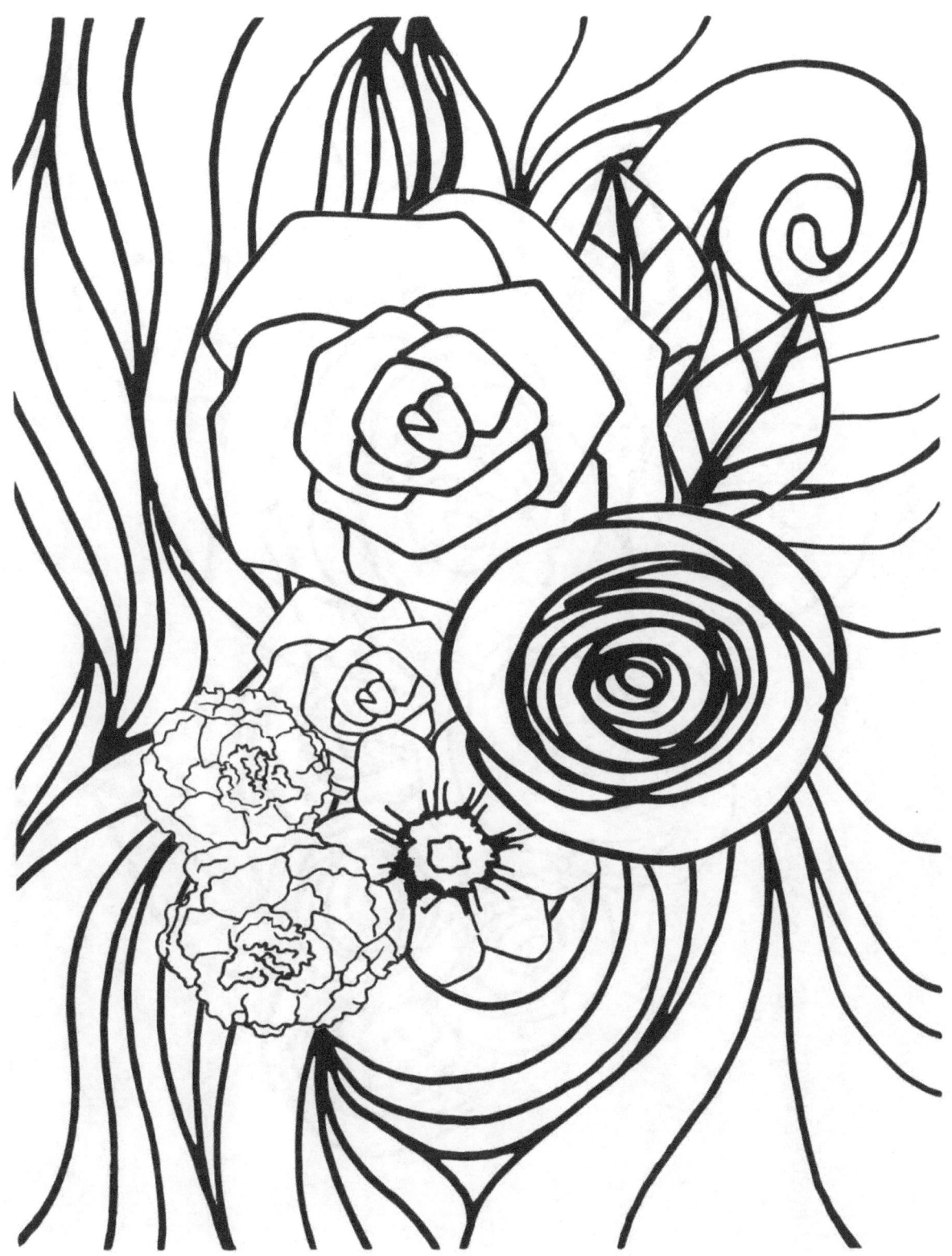

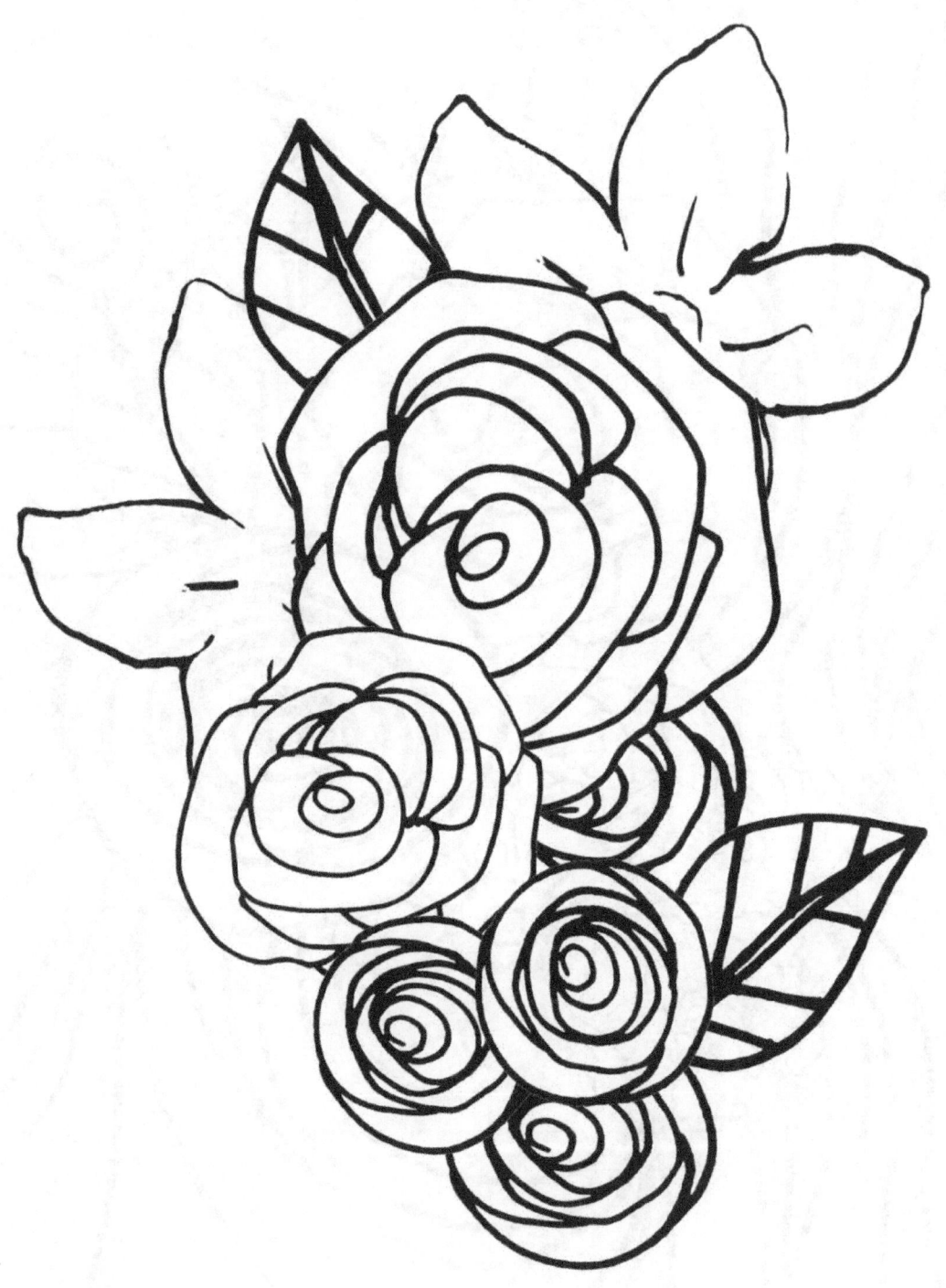

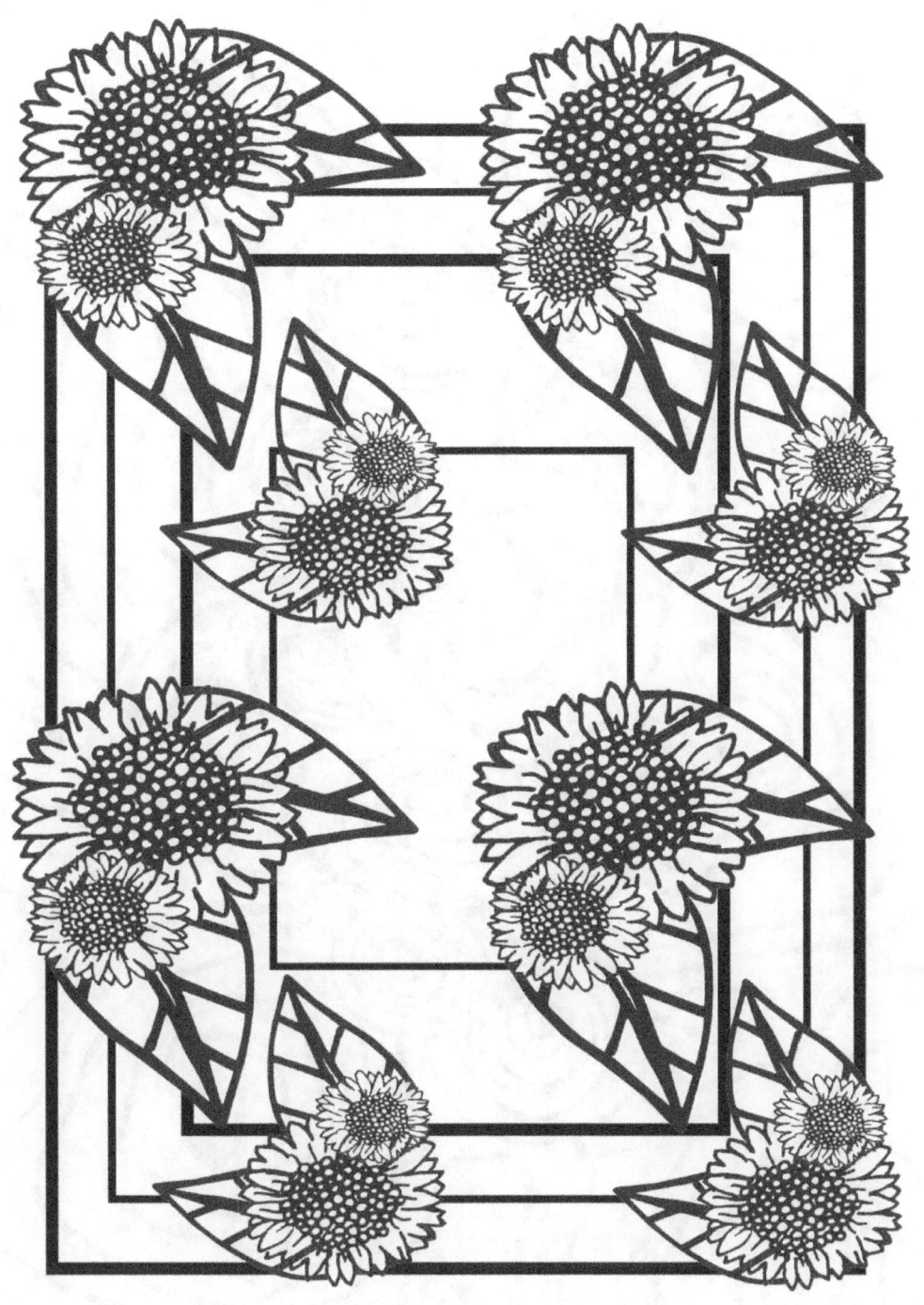

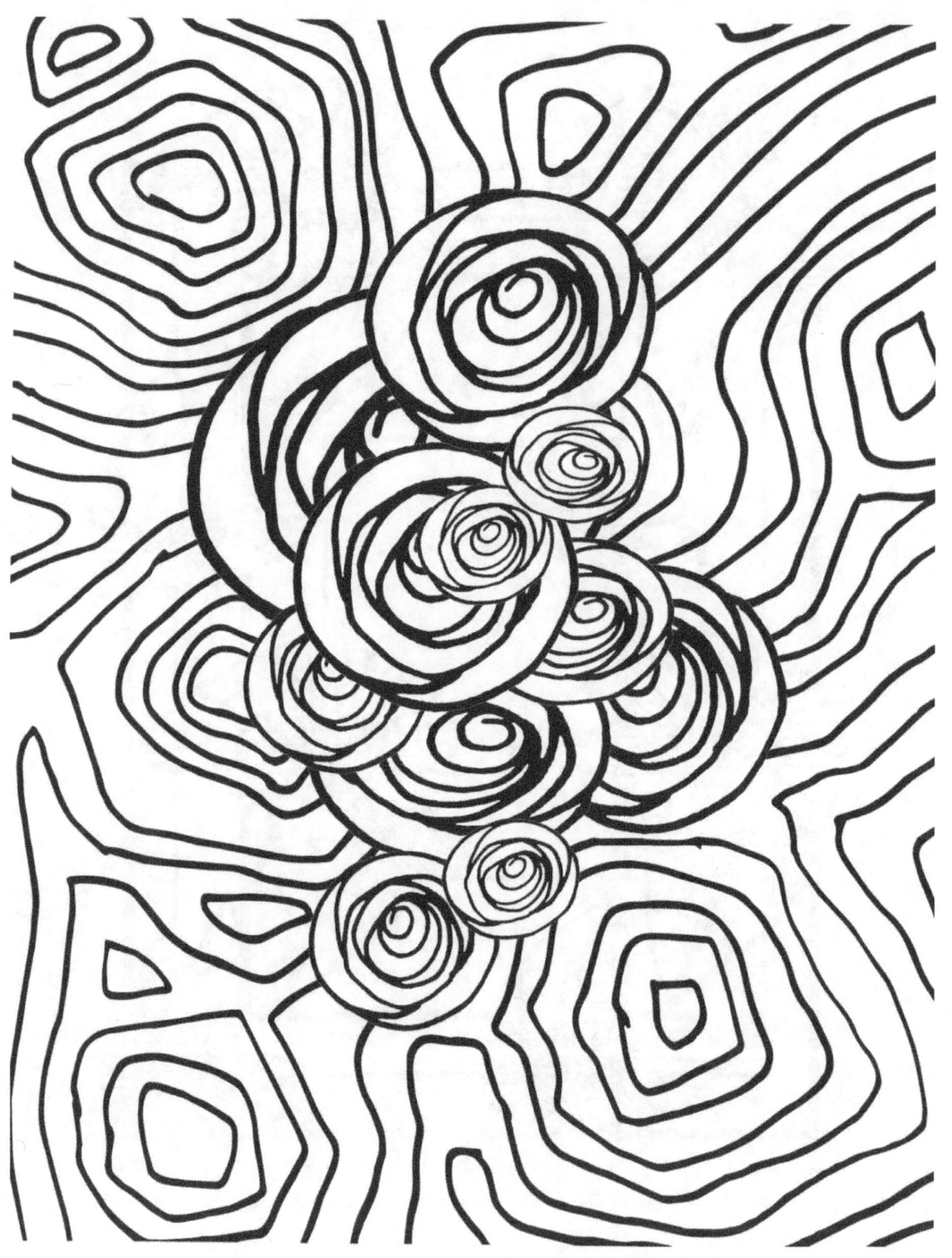

42

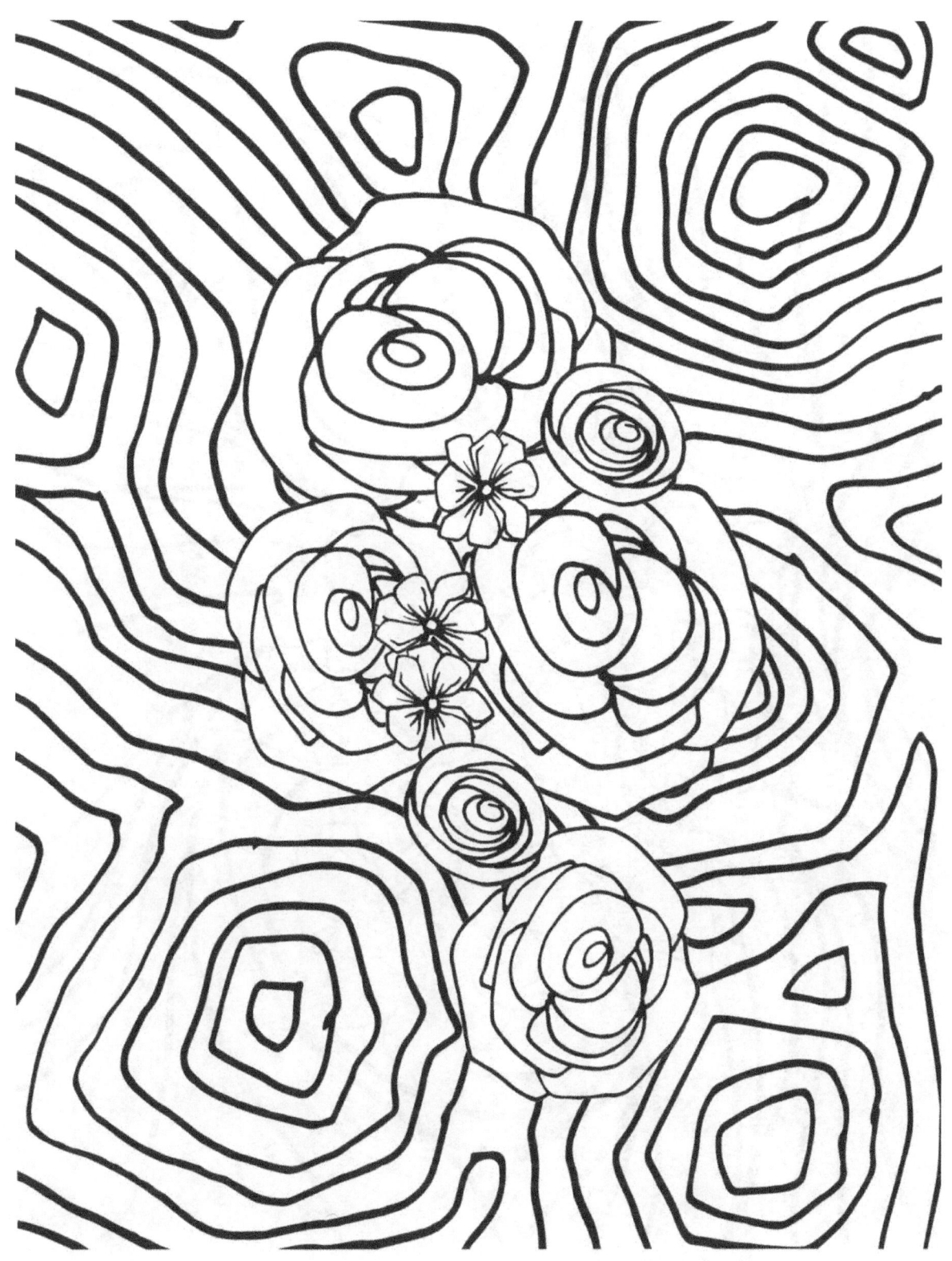

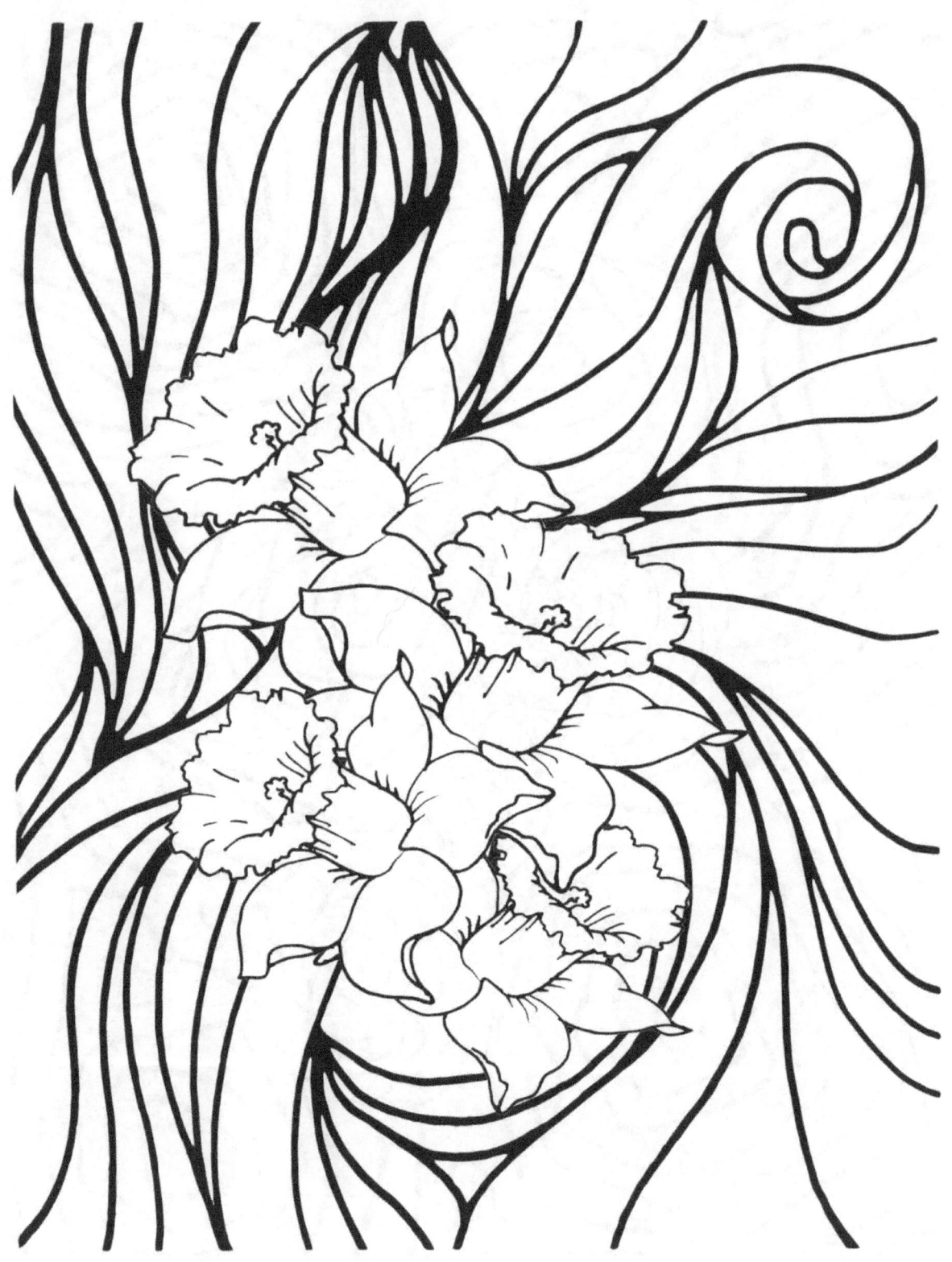

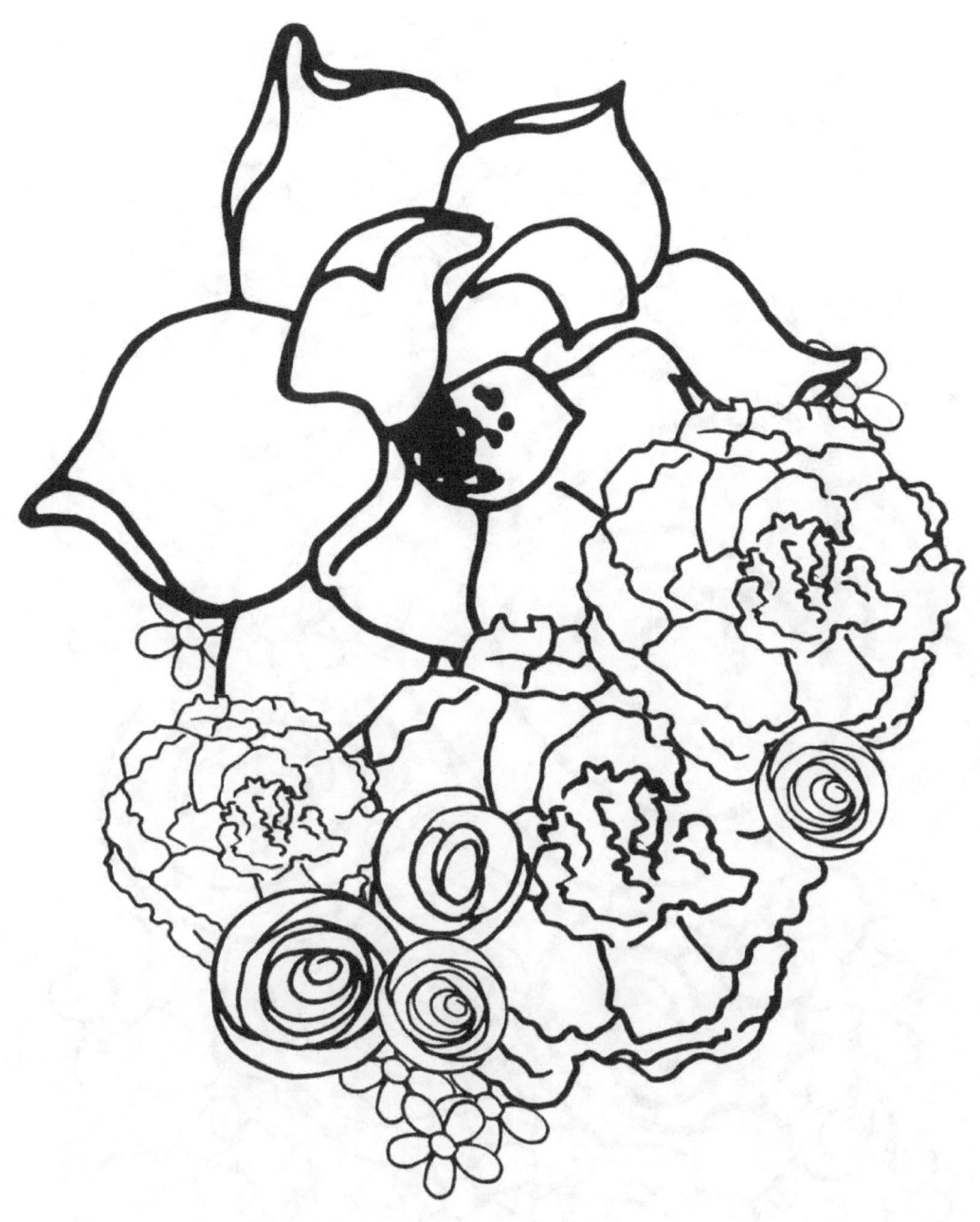

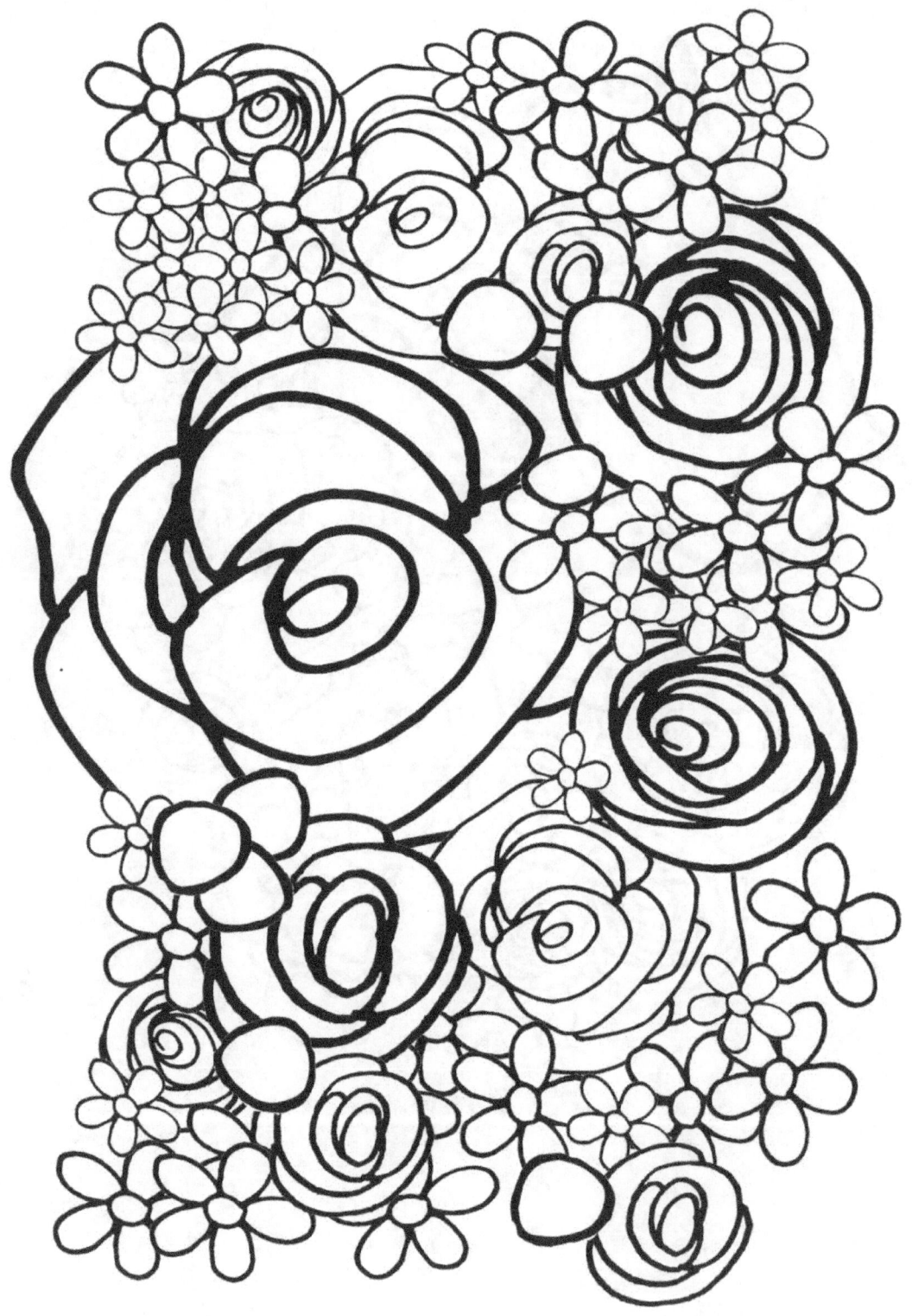

46

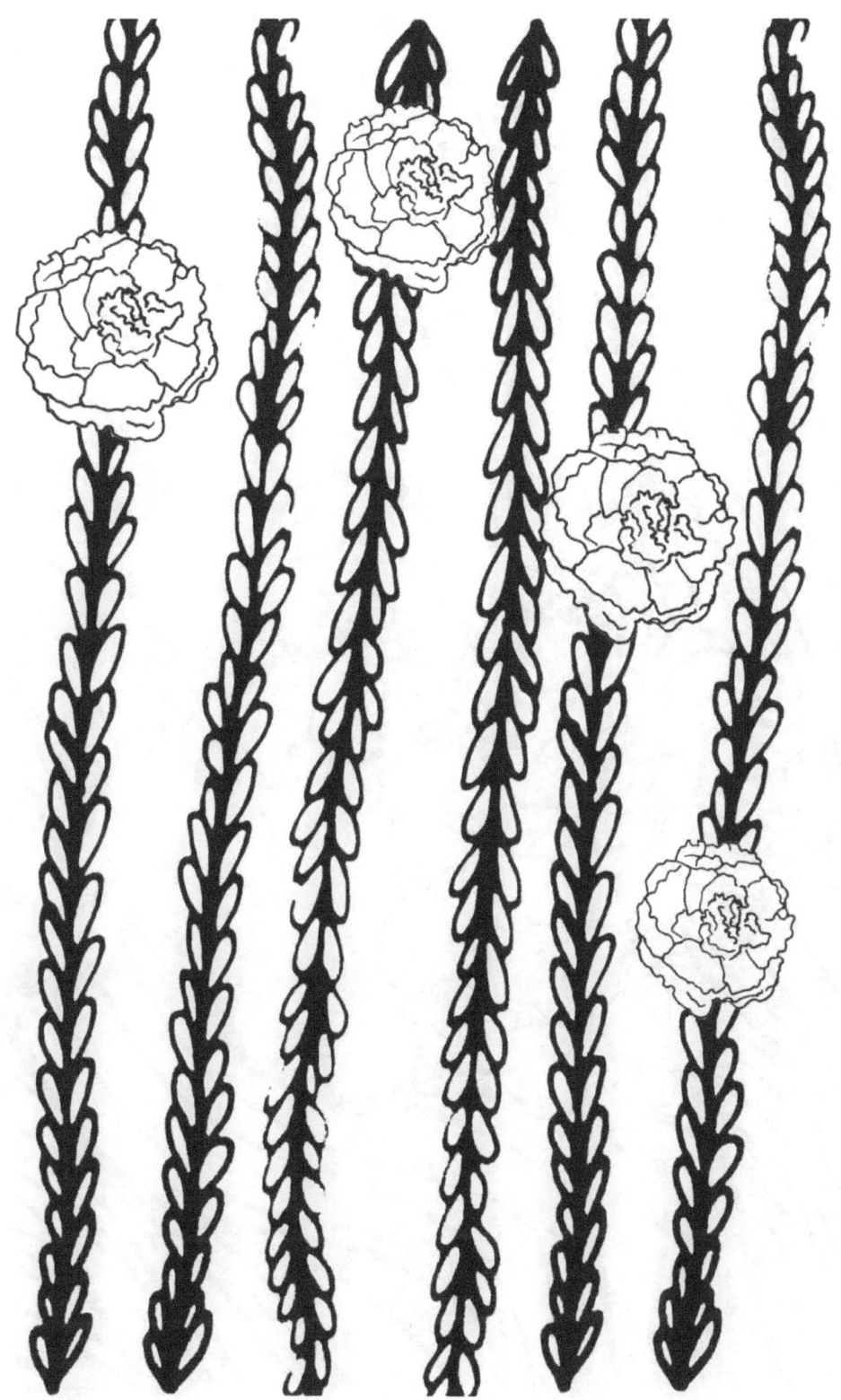

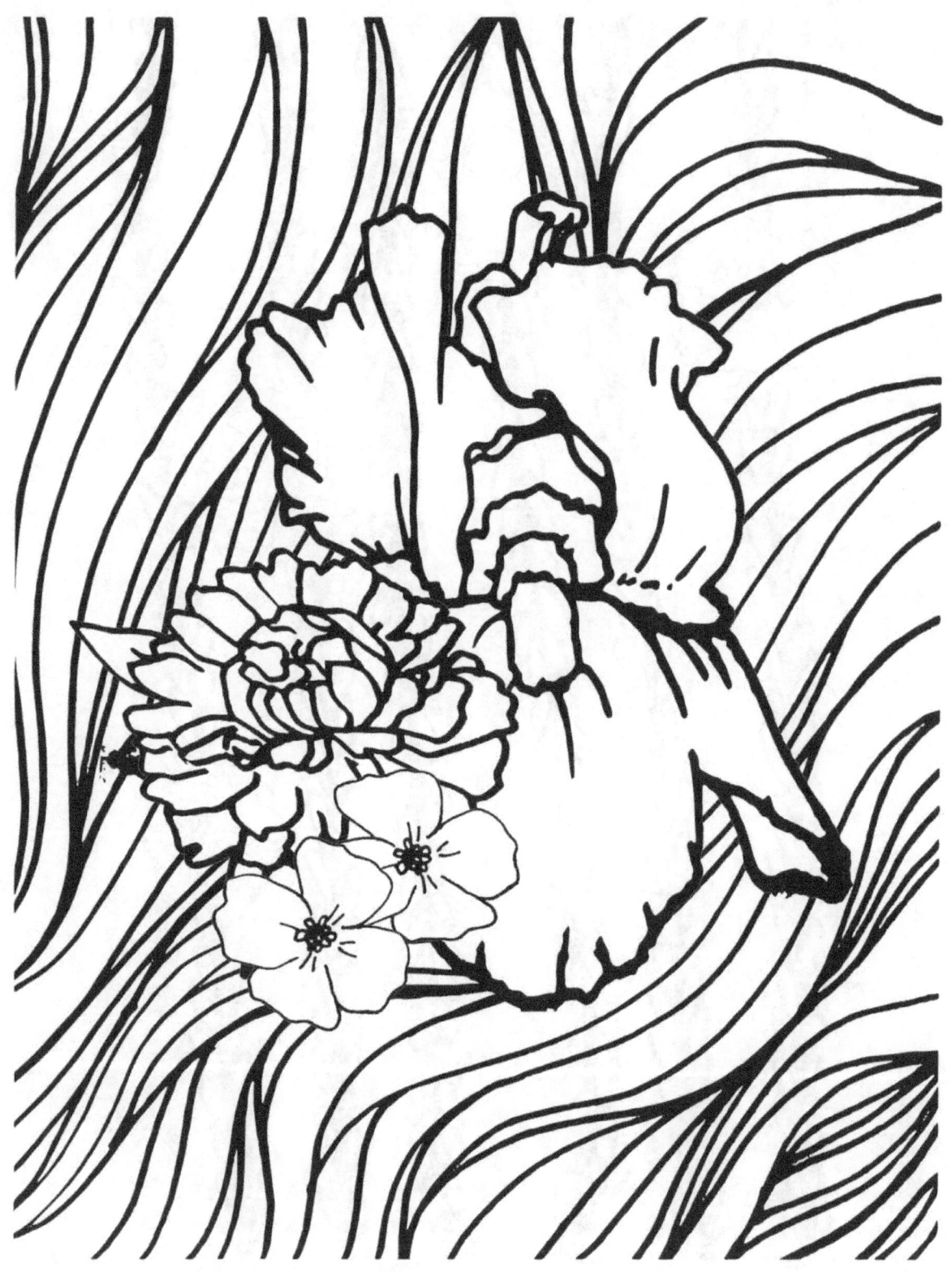

48

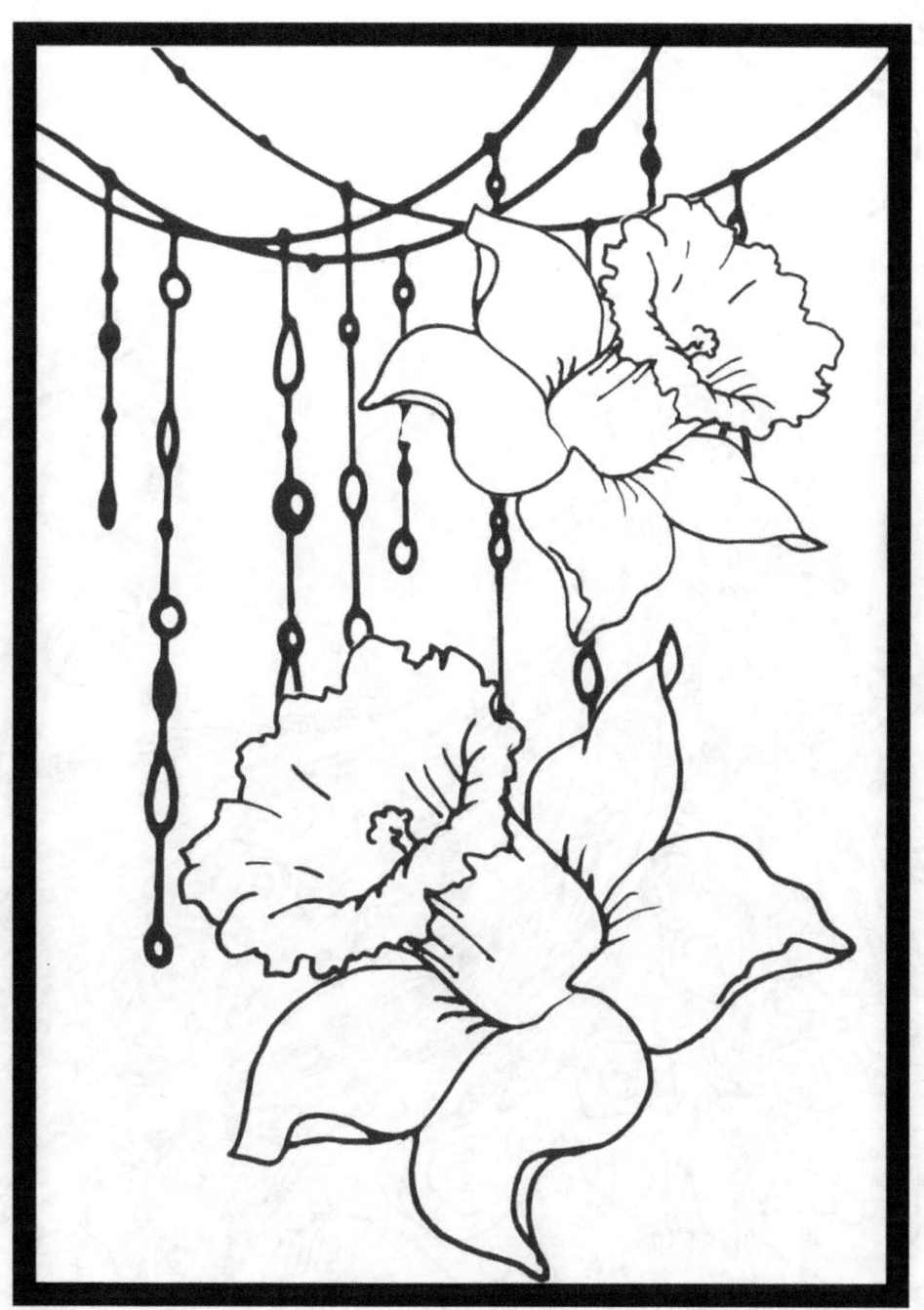

49

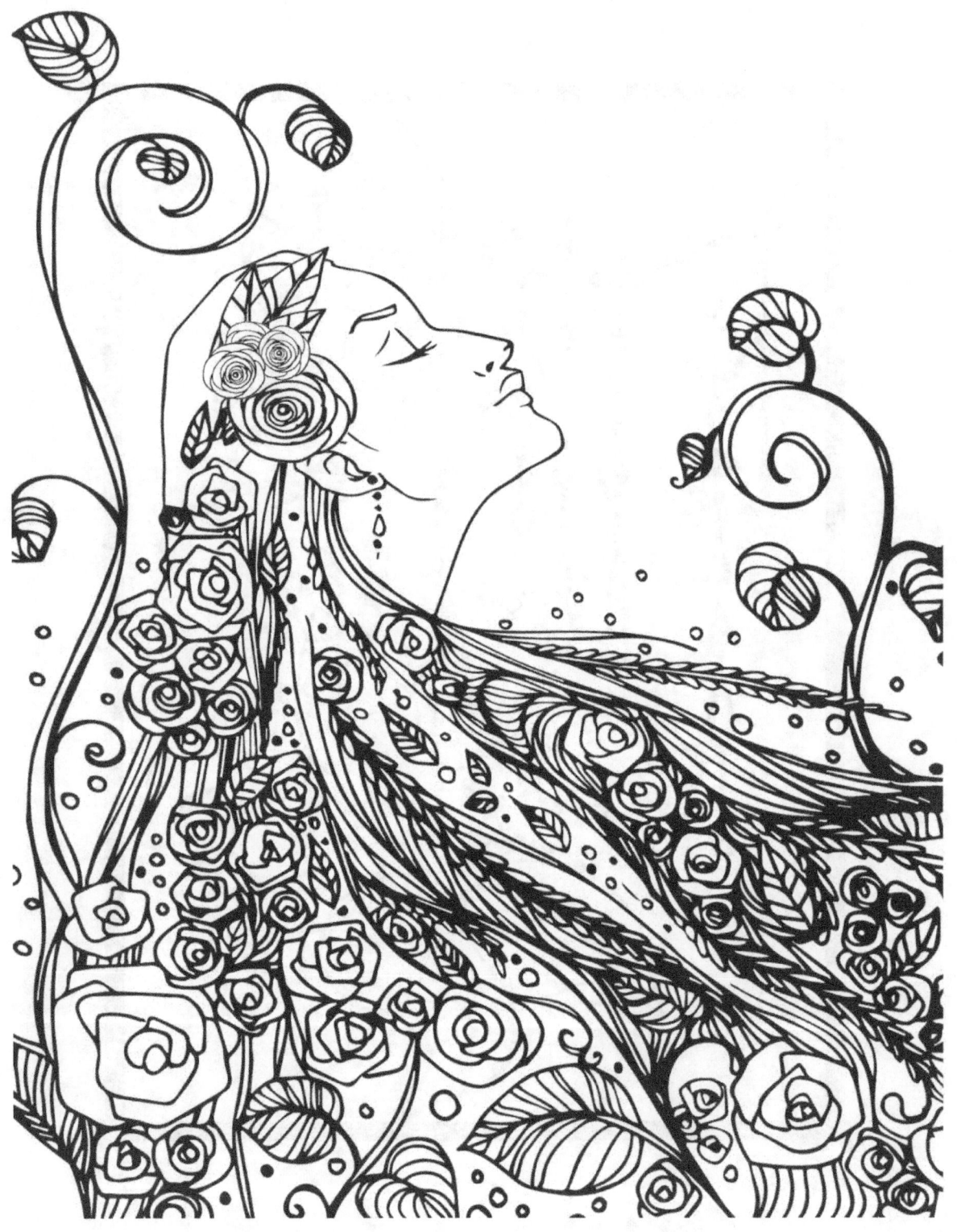

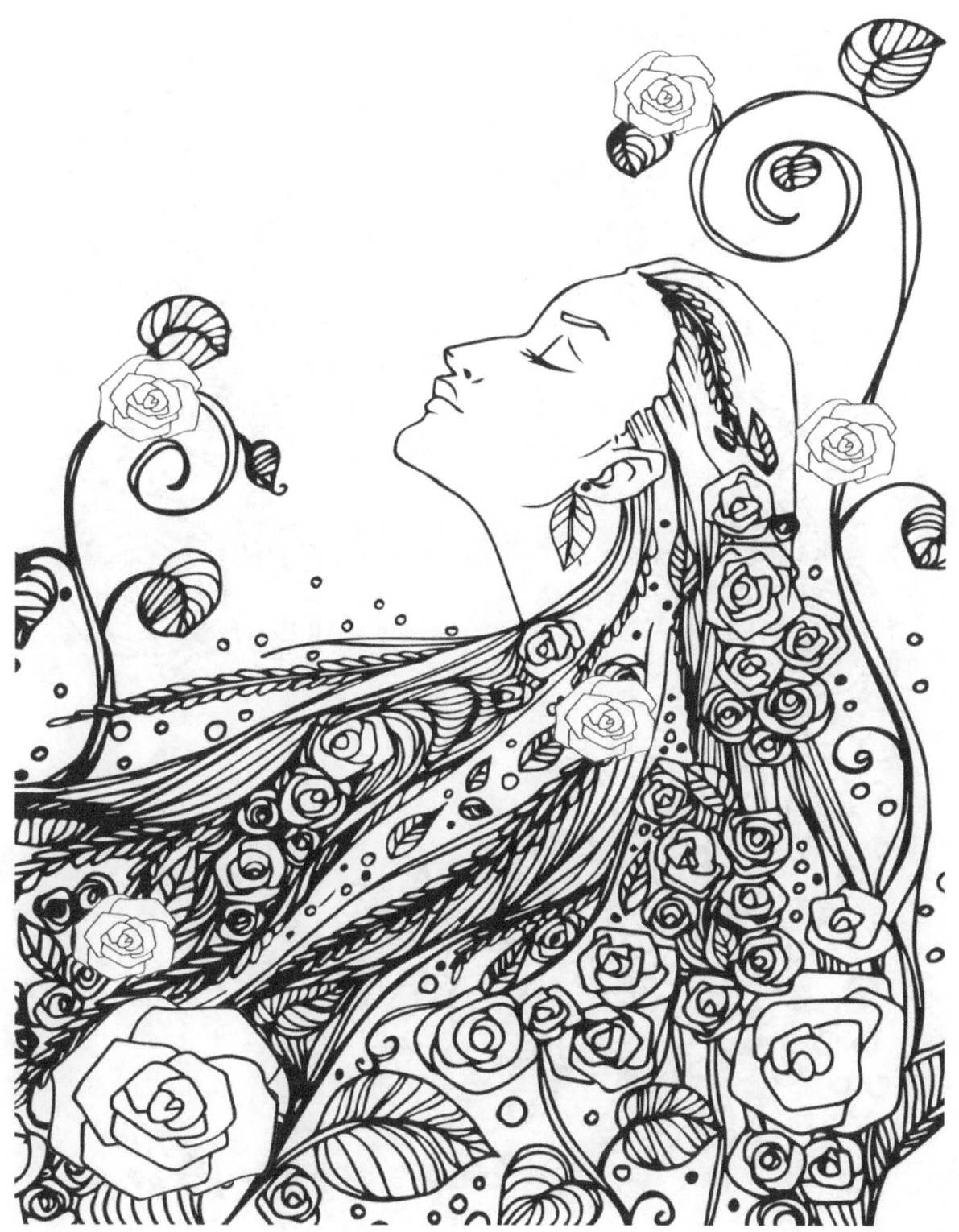

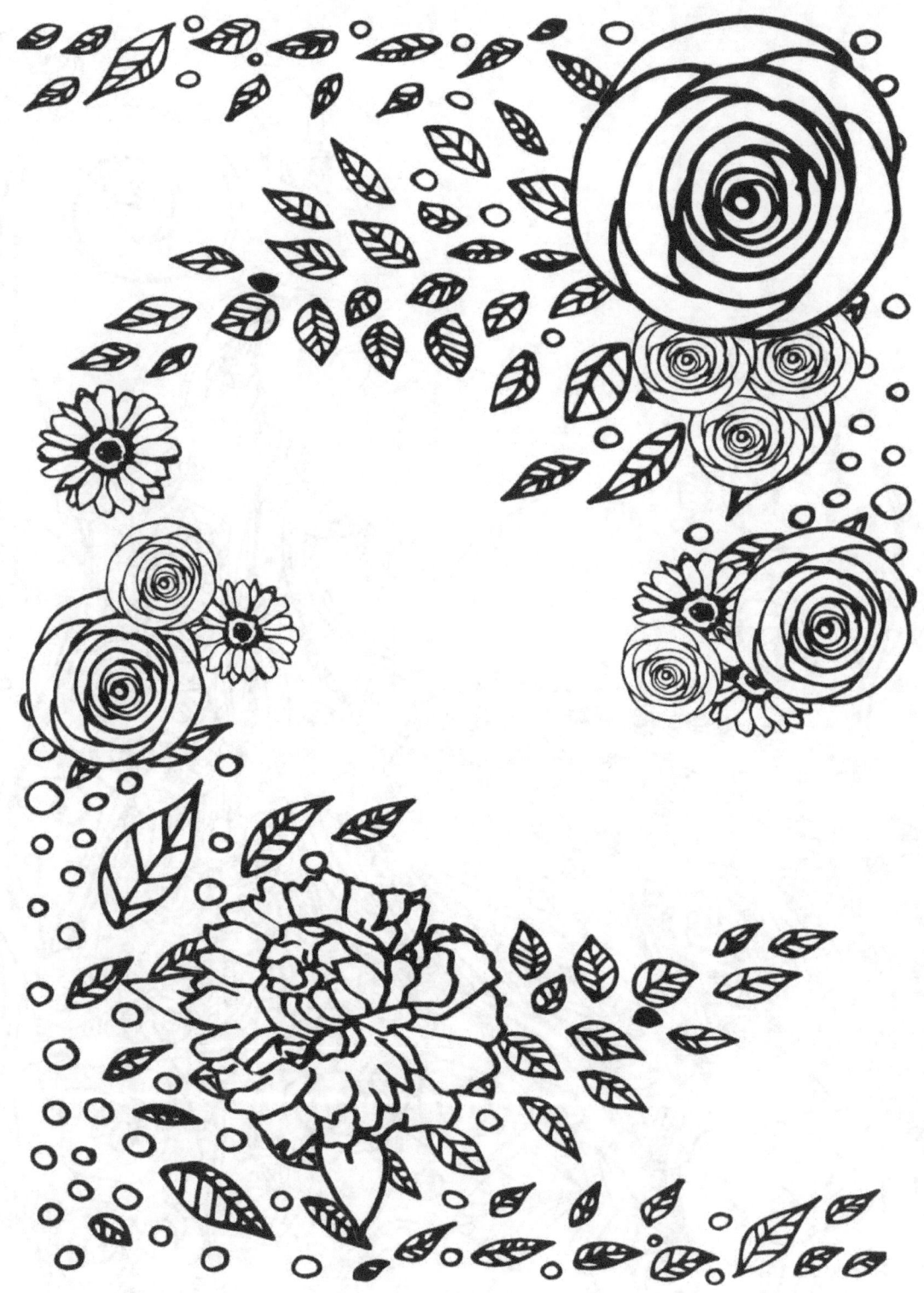

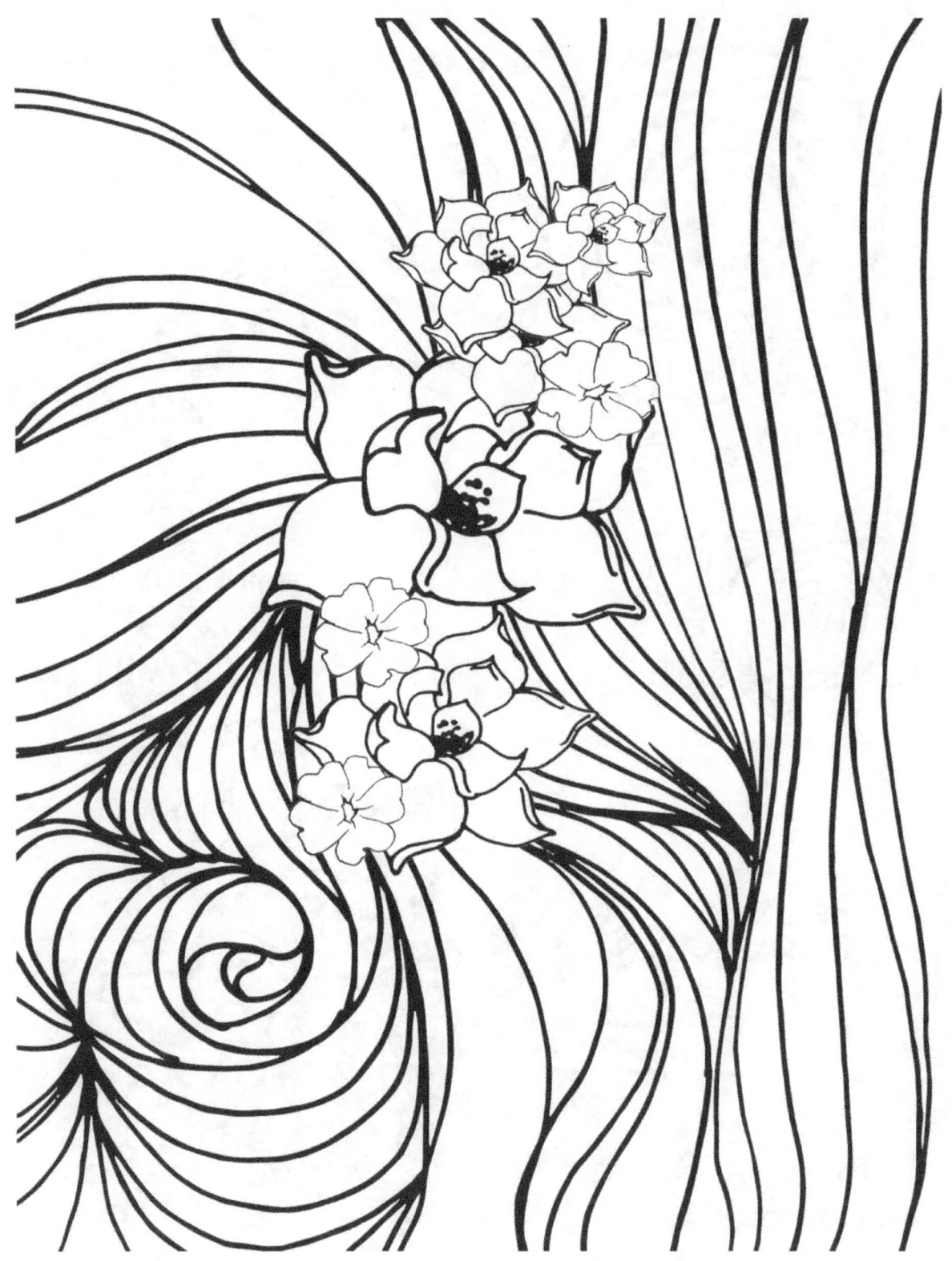

54

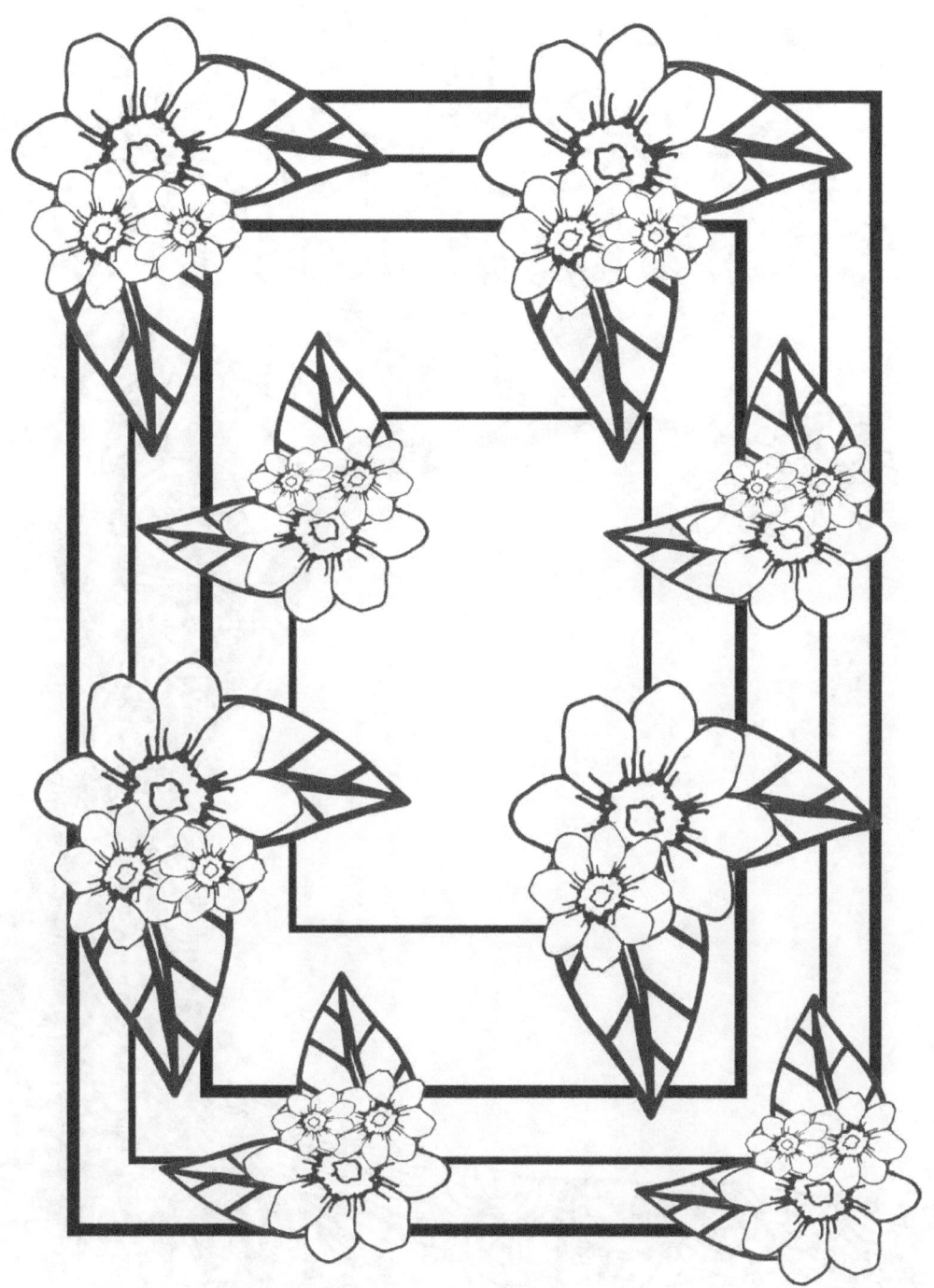

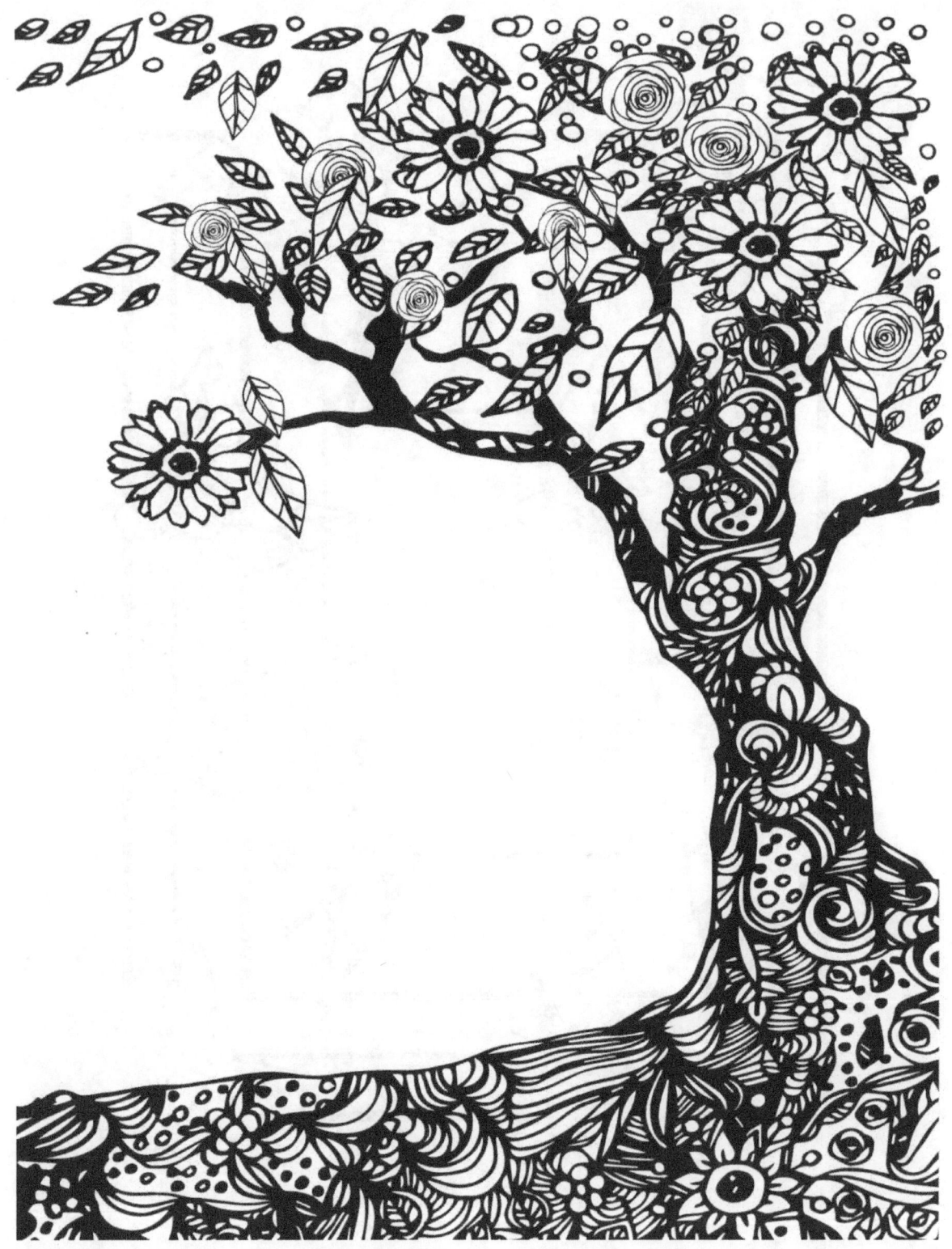

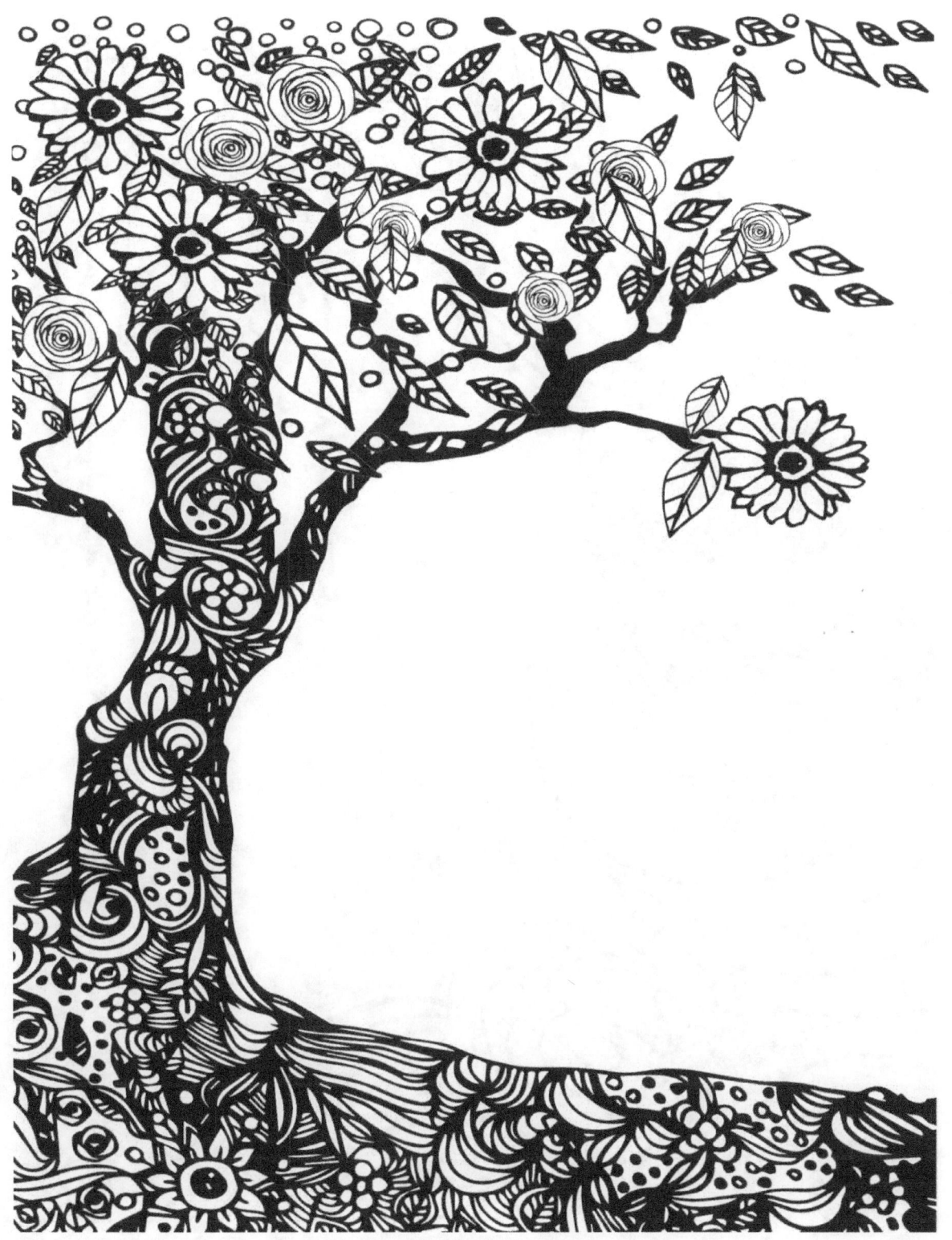

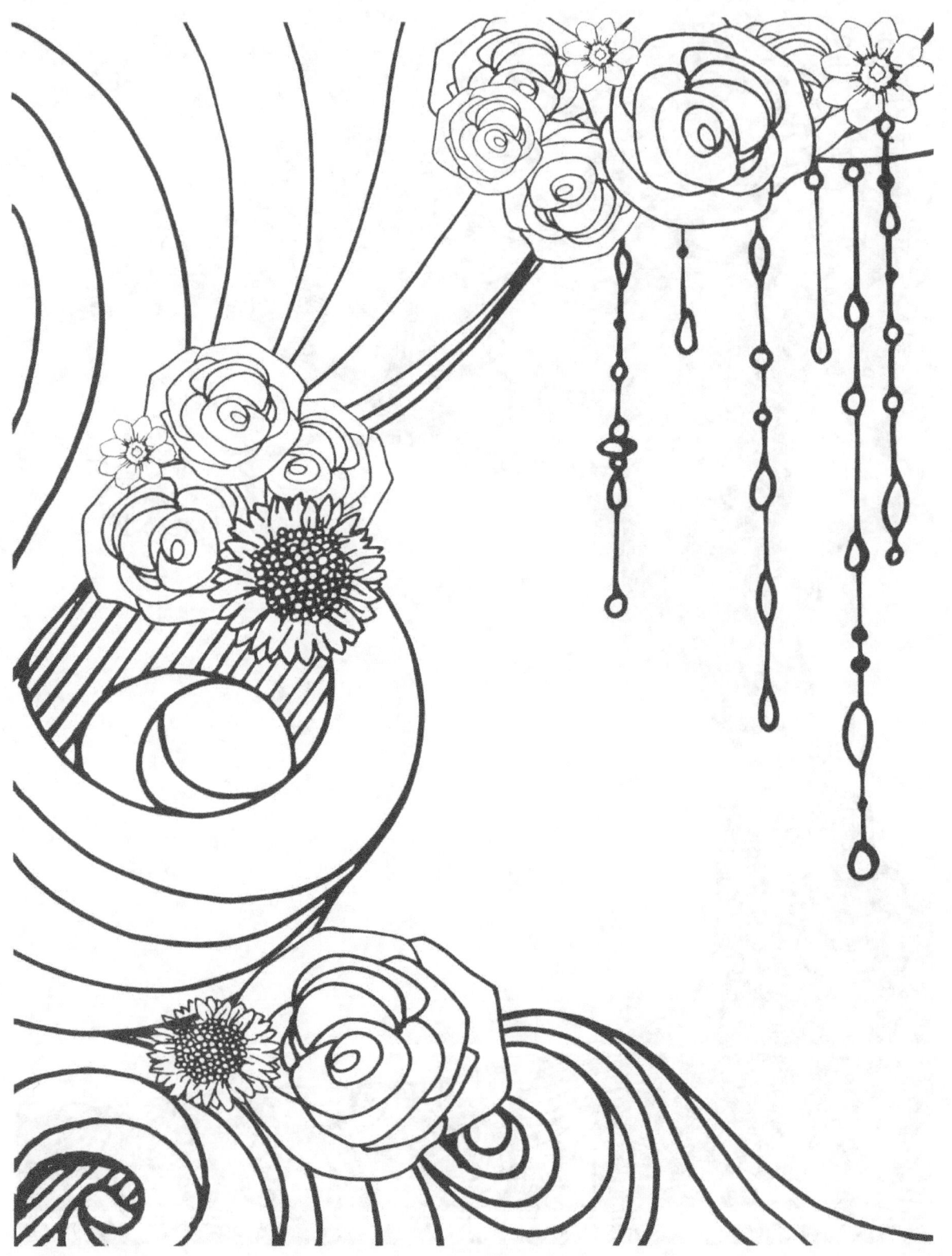

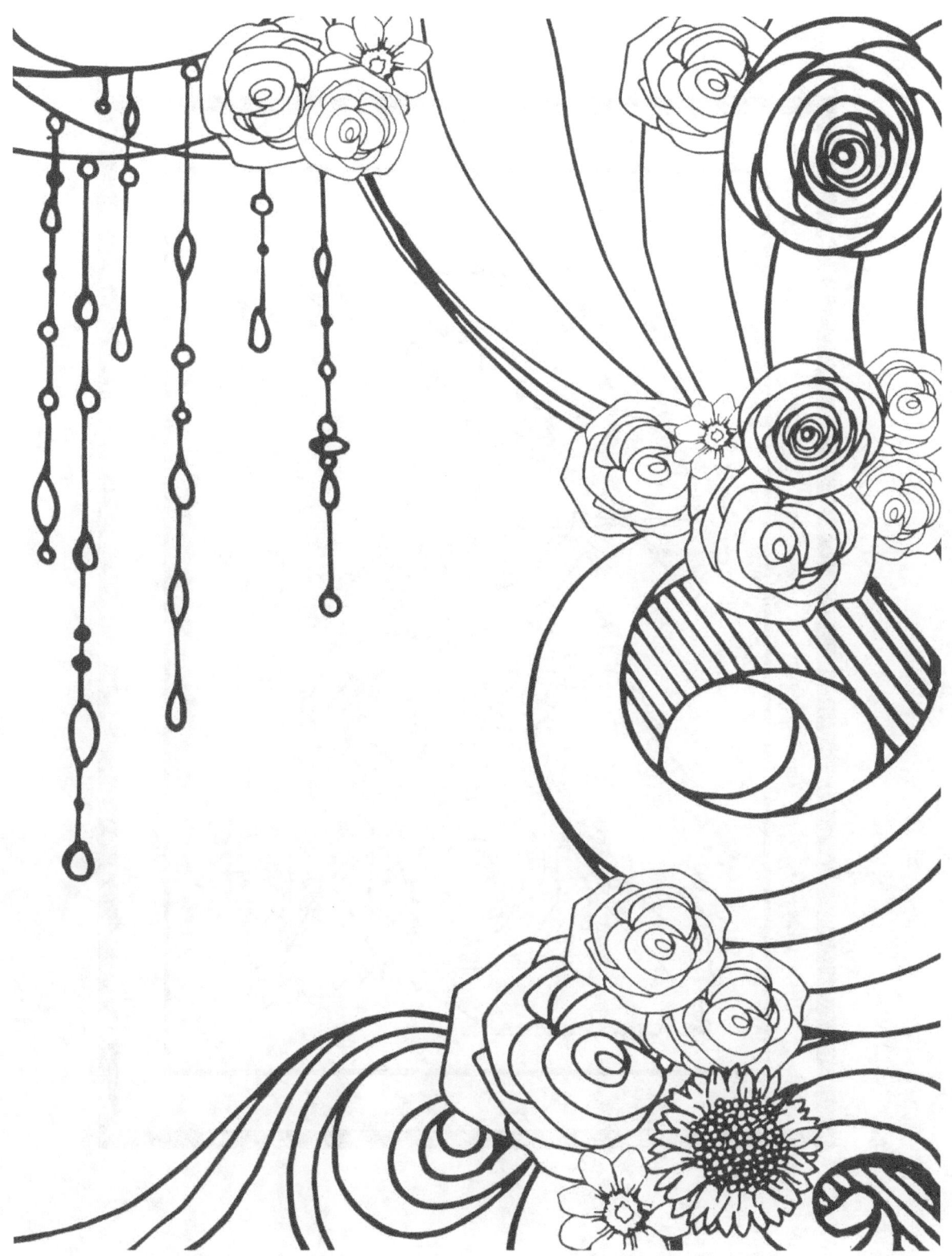

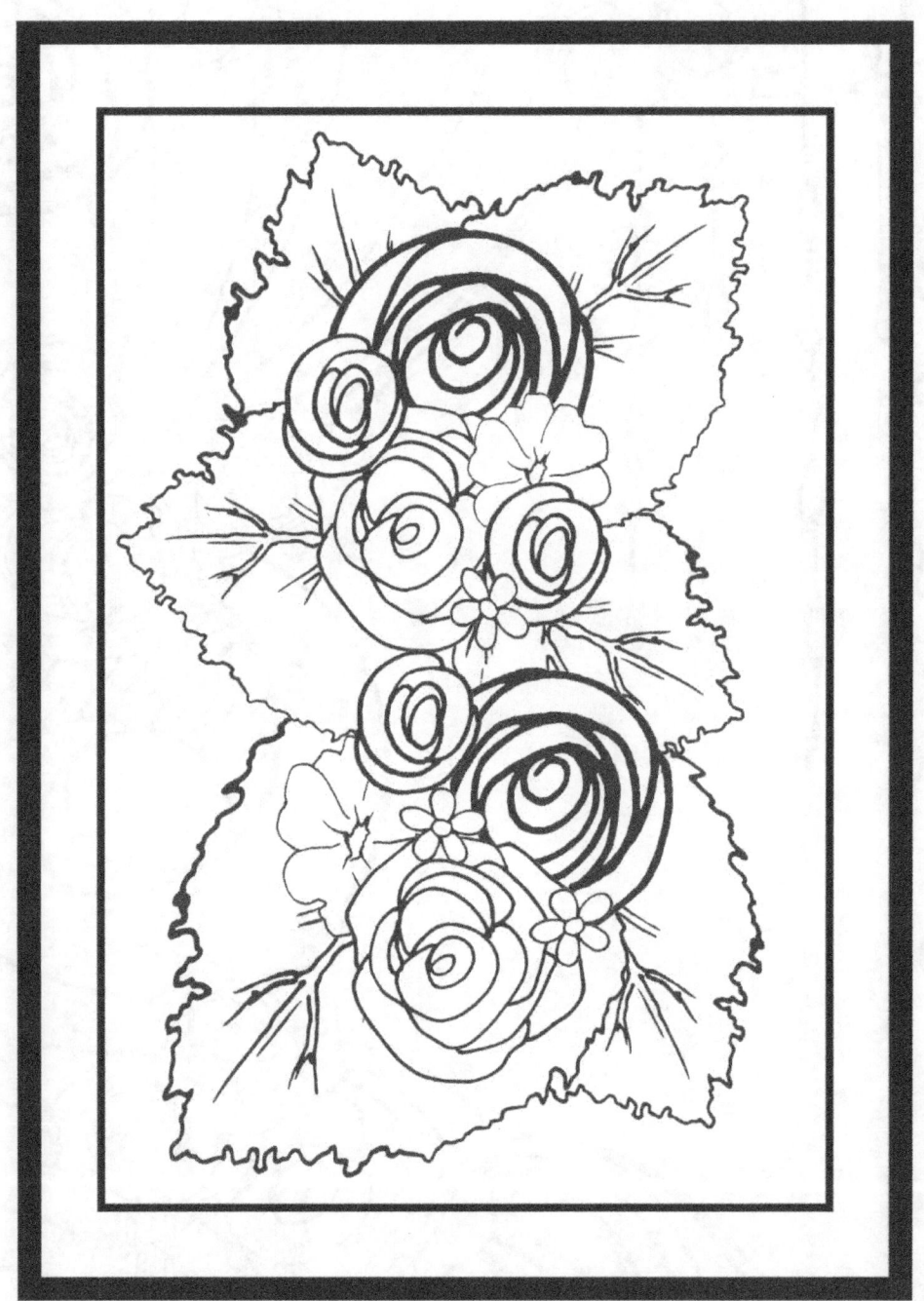

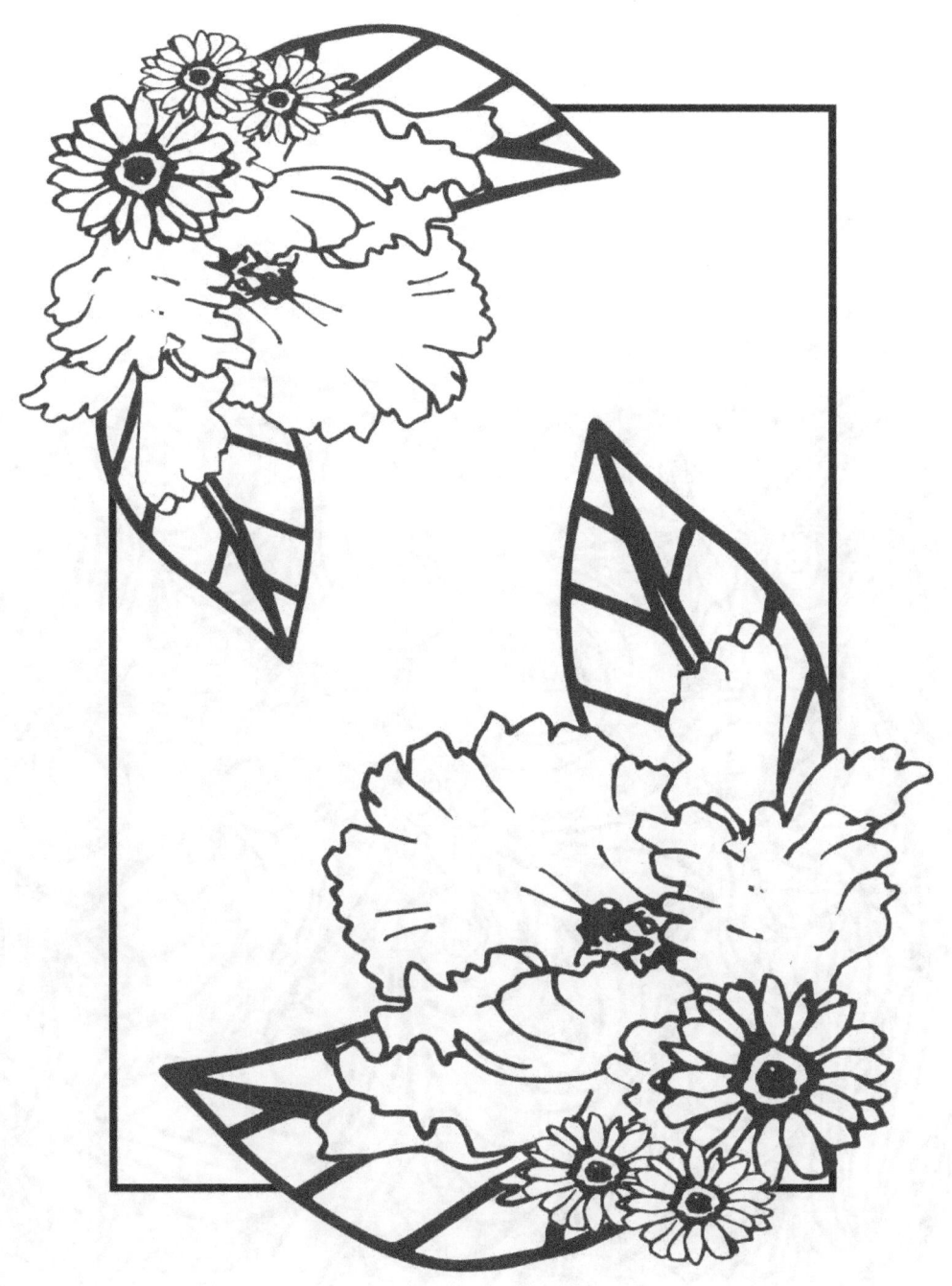

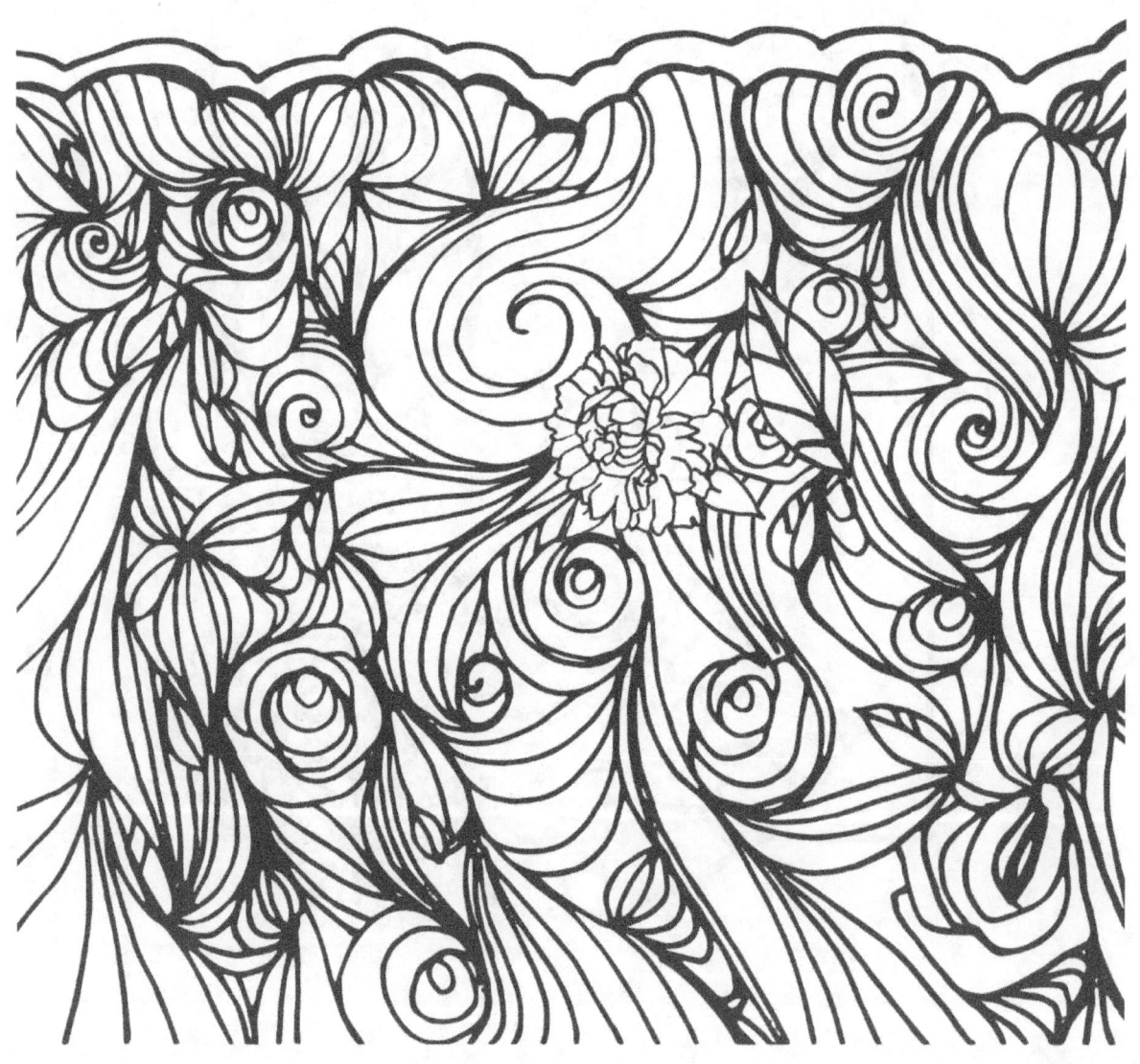

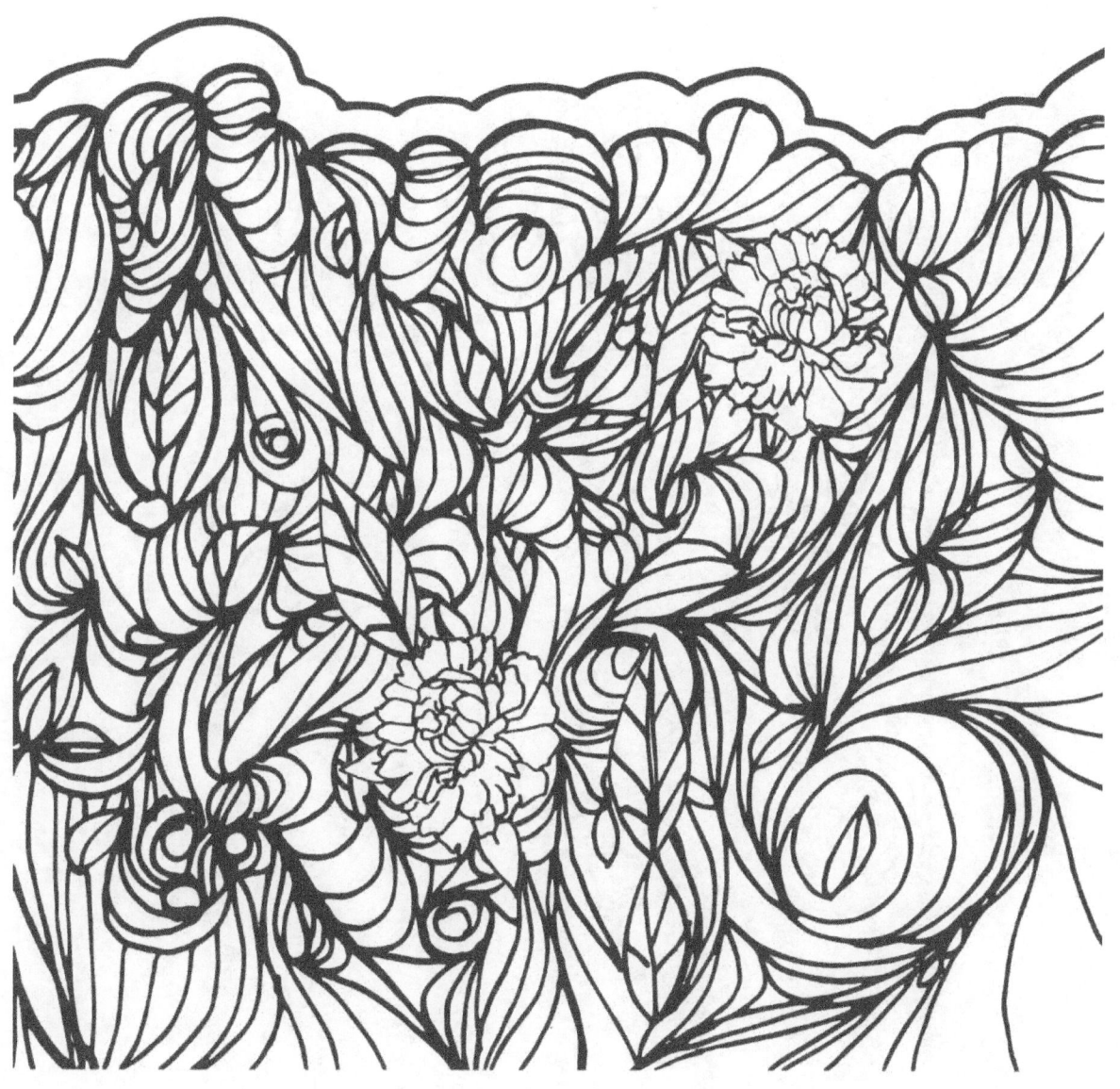

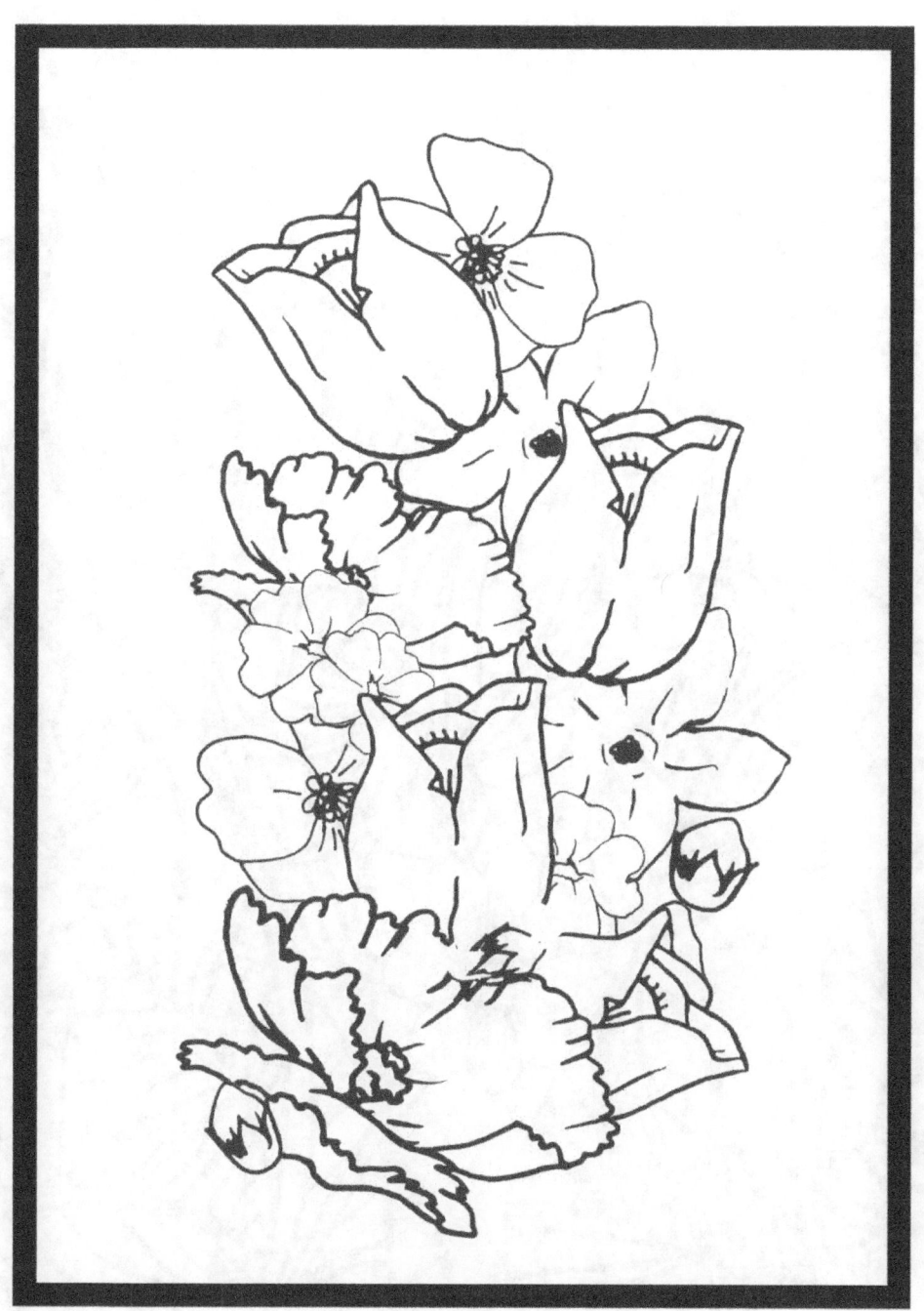

65

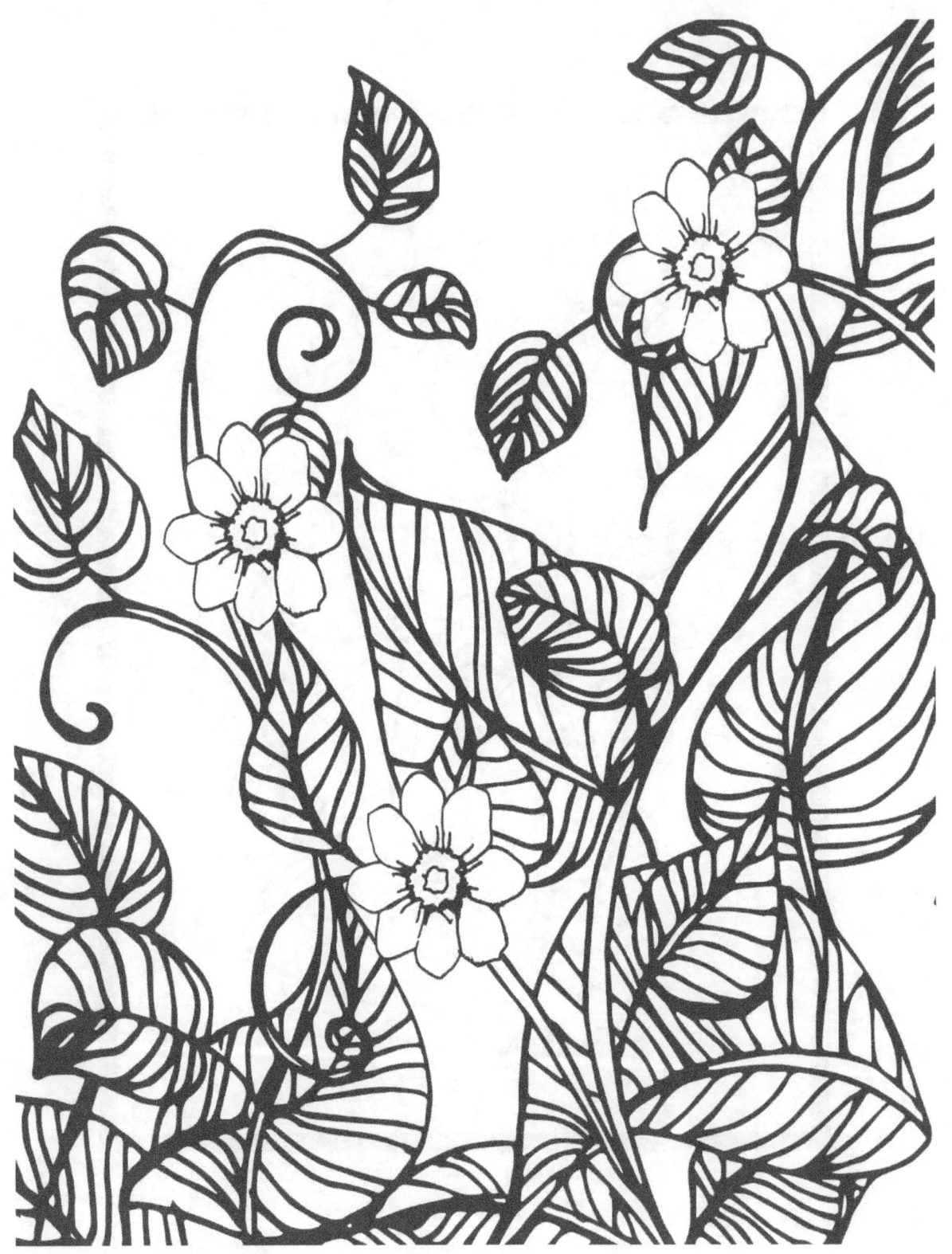

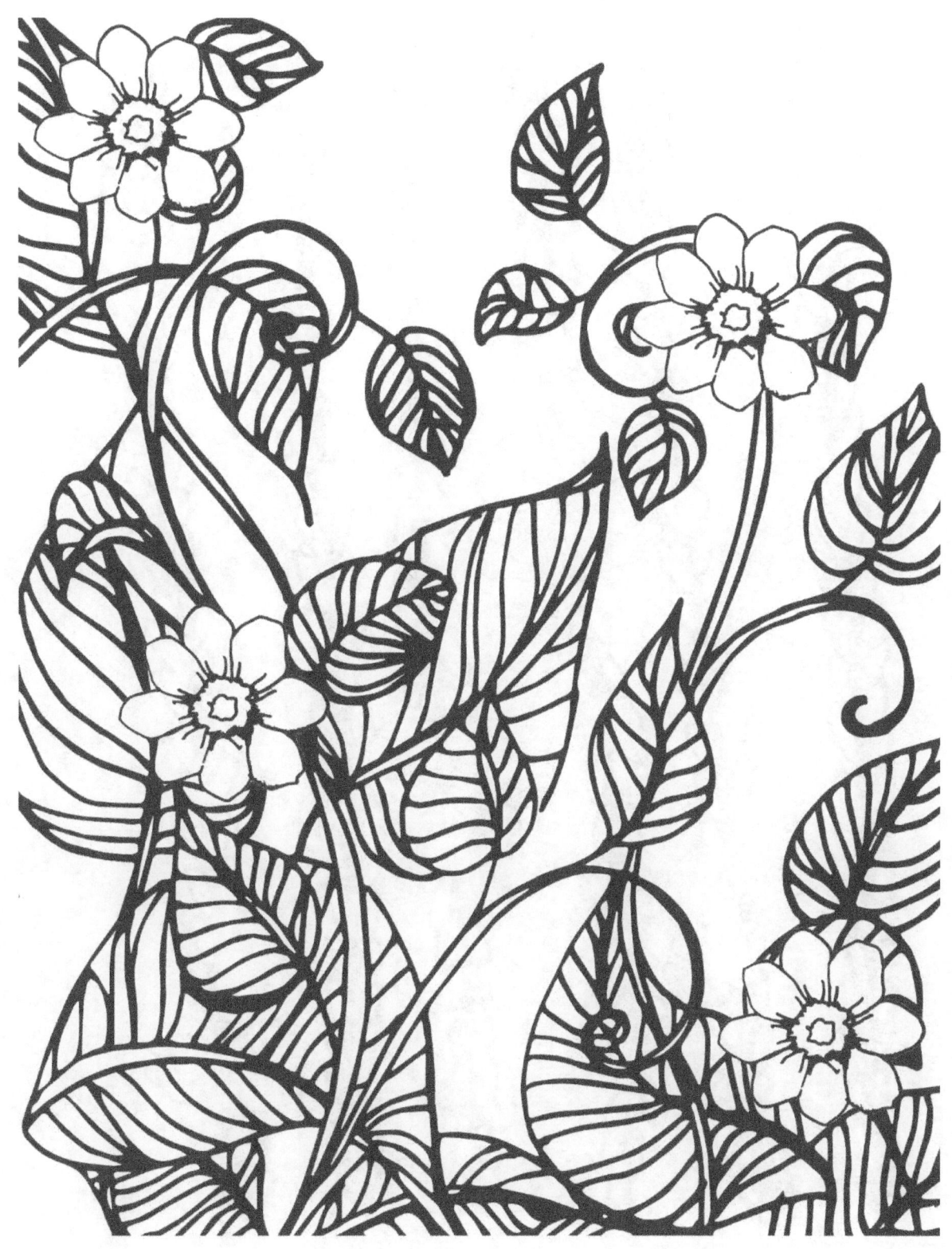

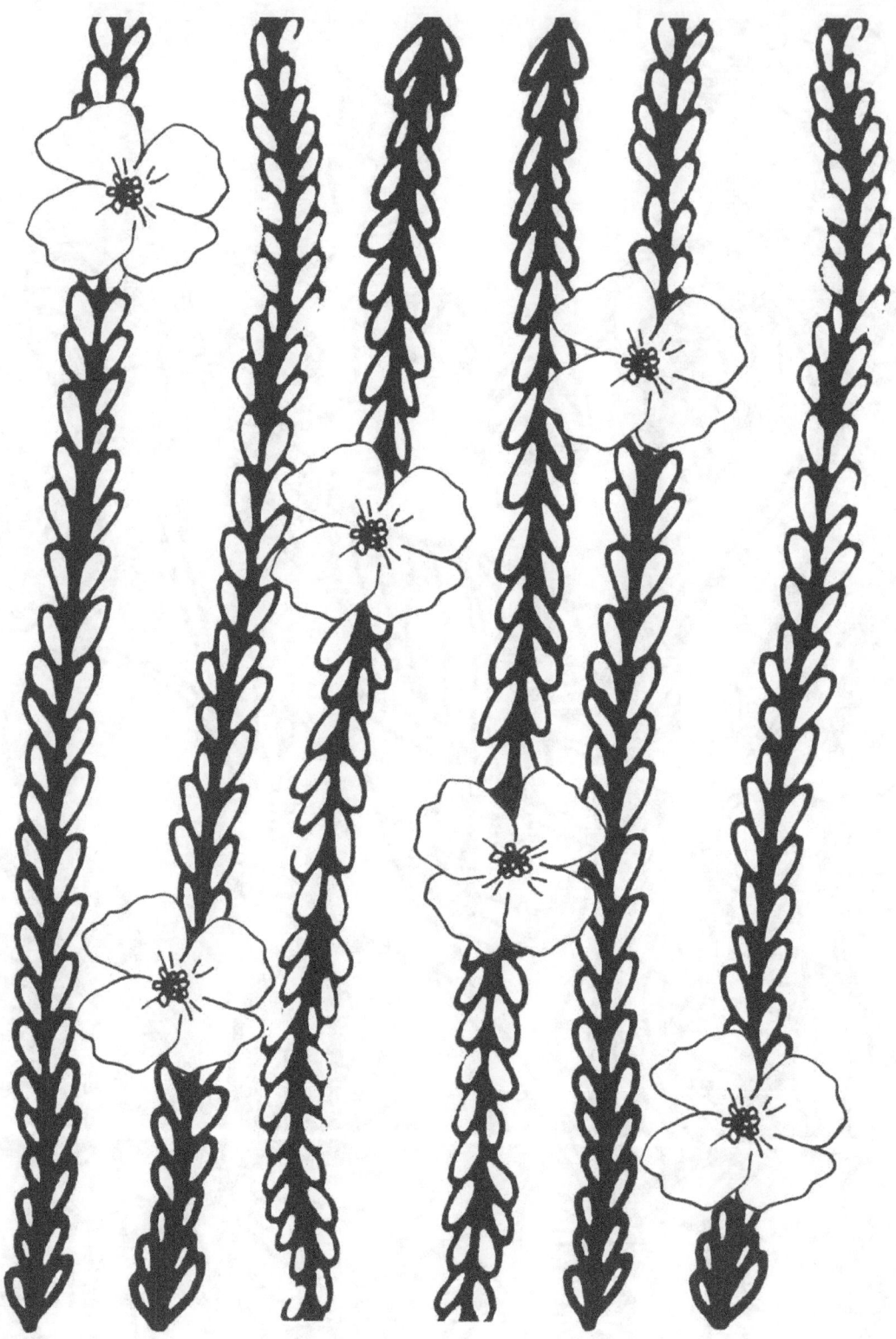

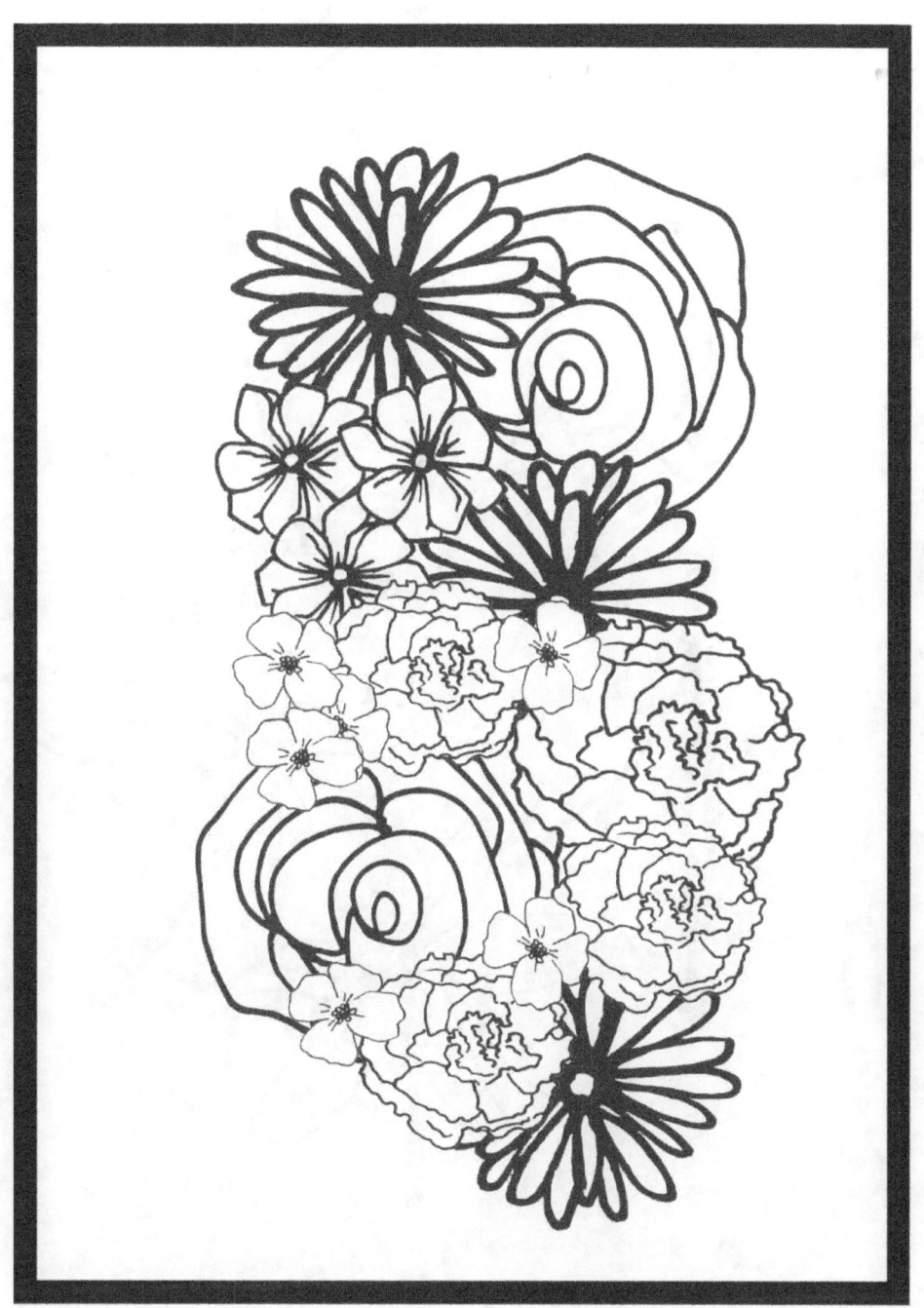

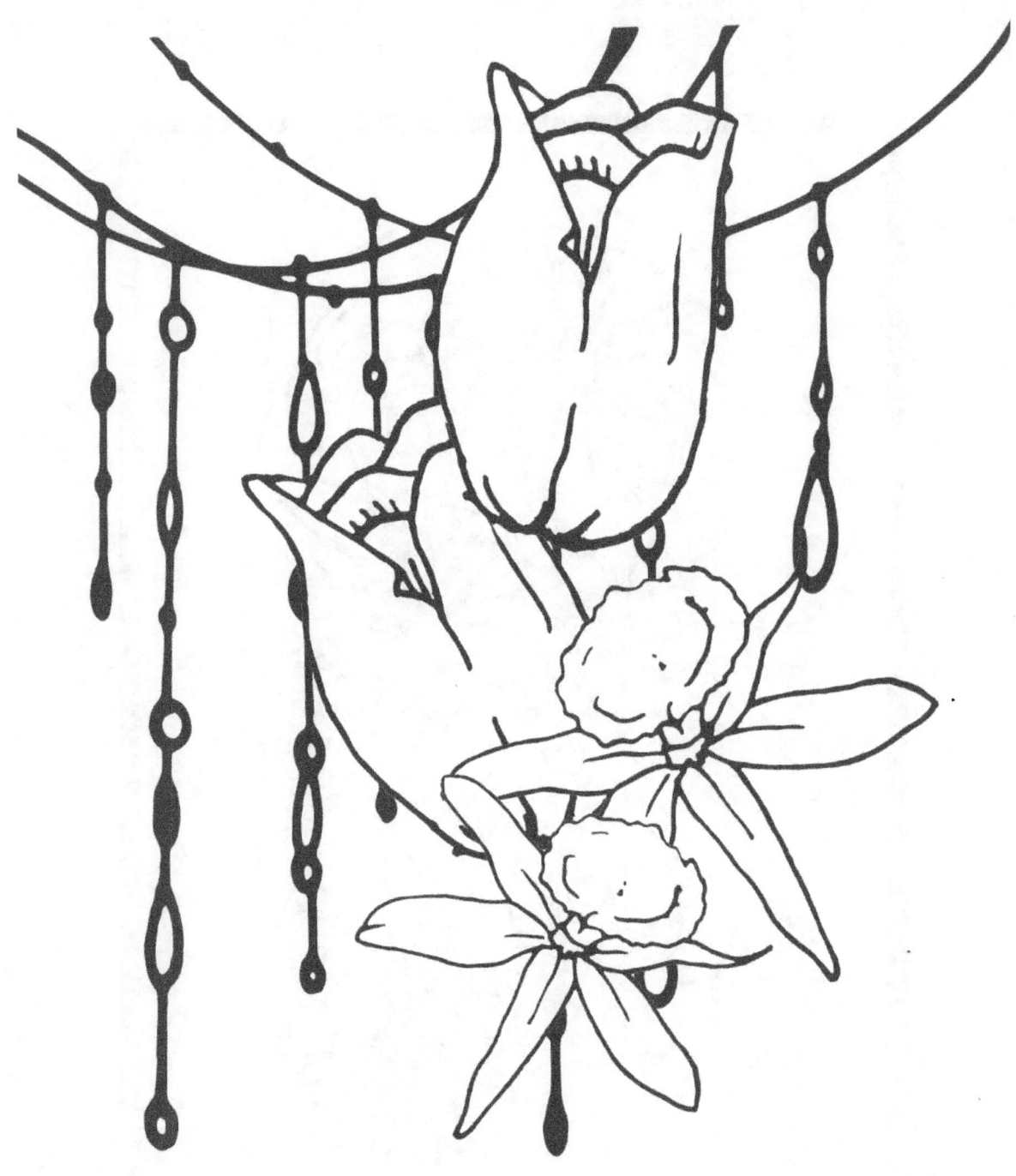

70

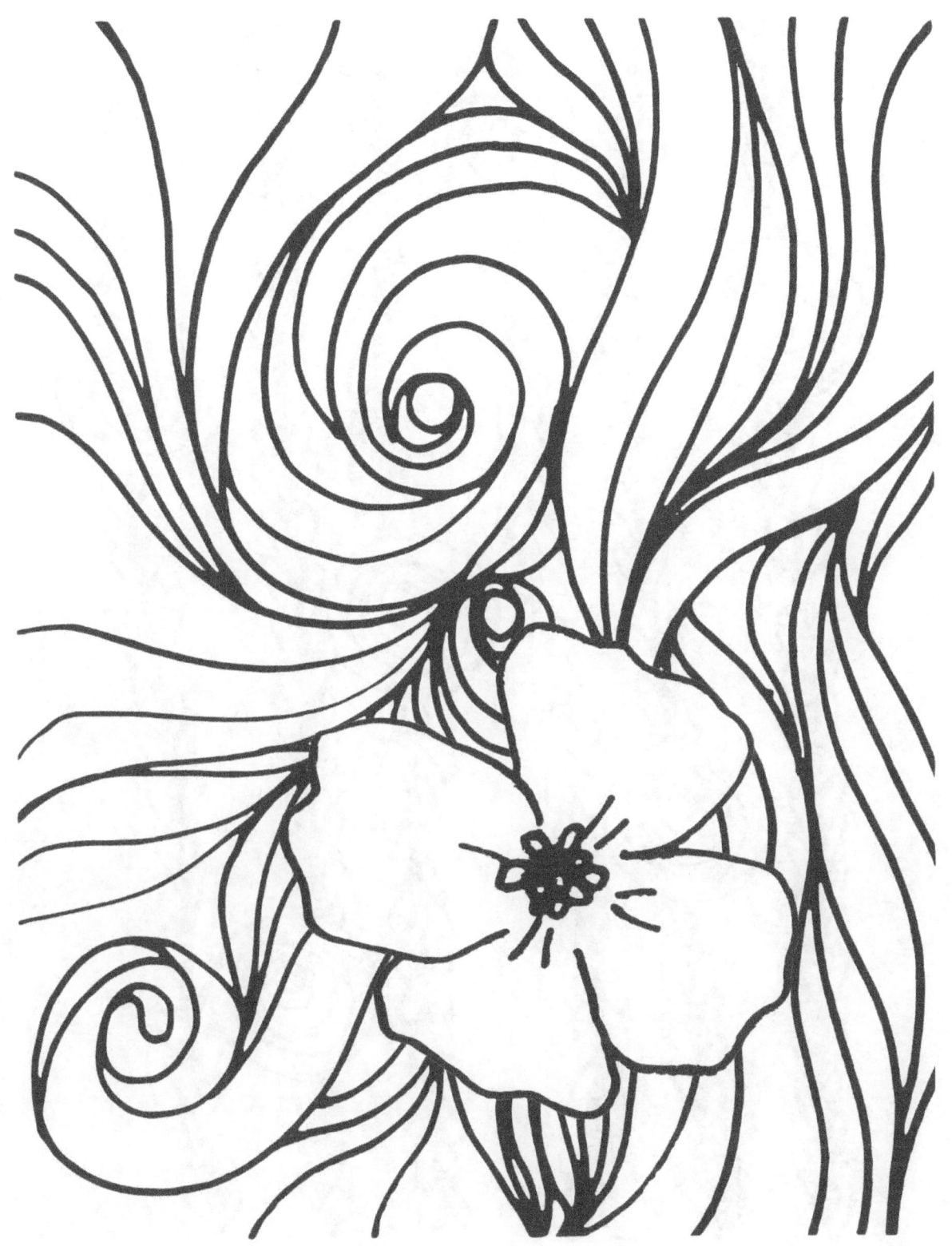

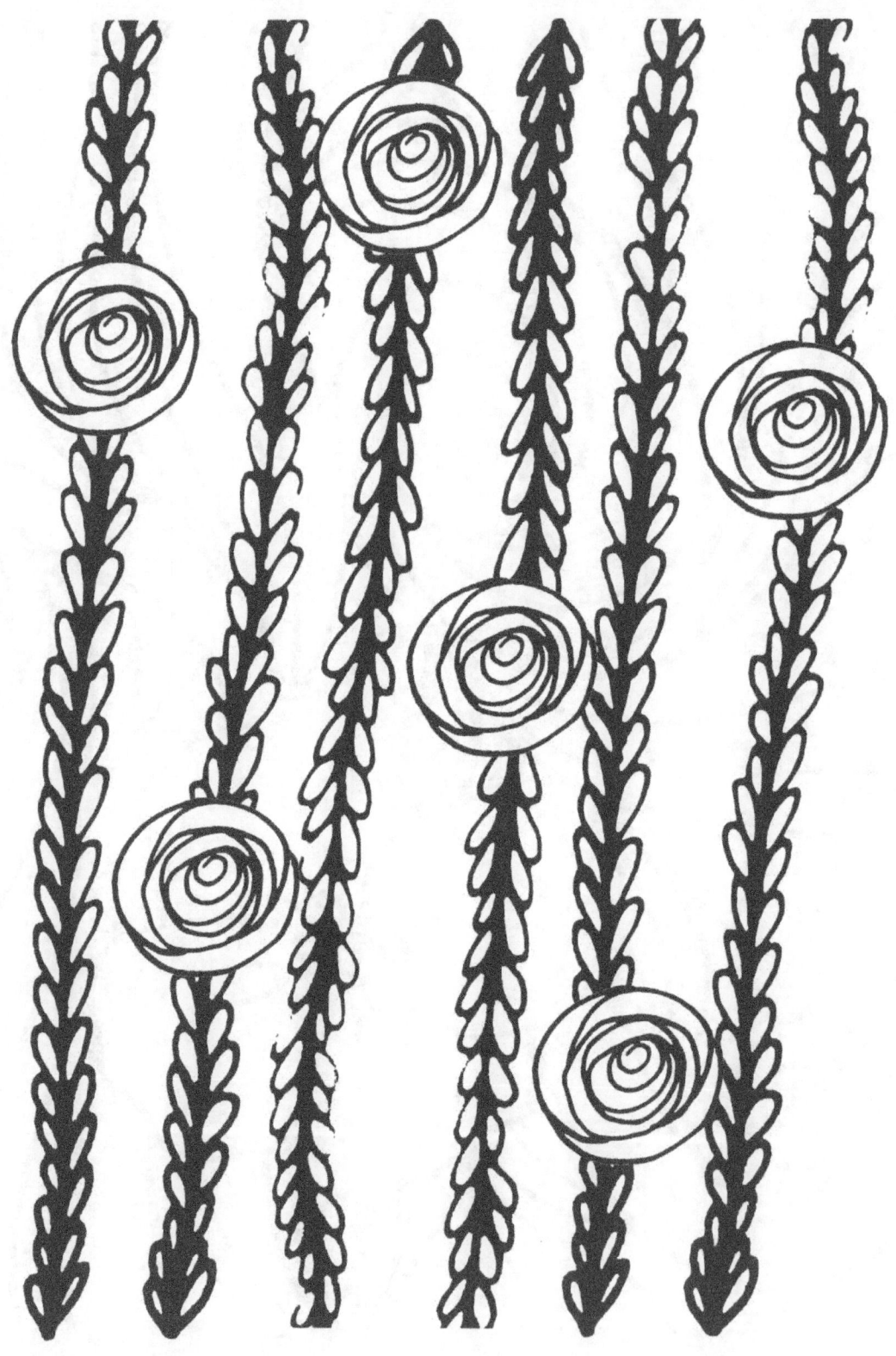

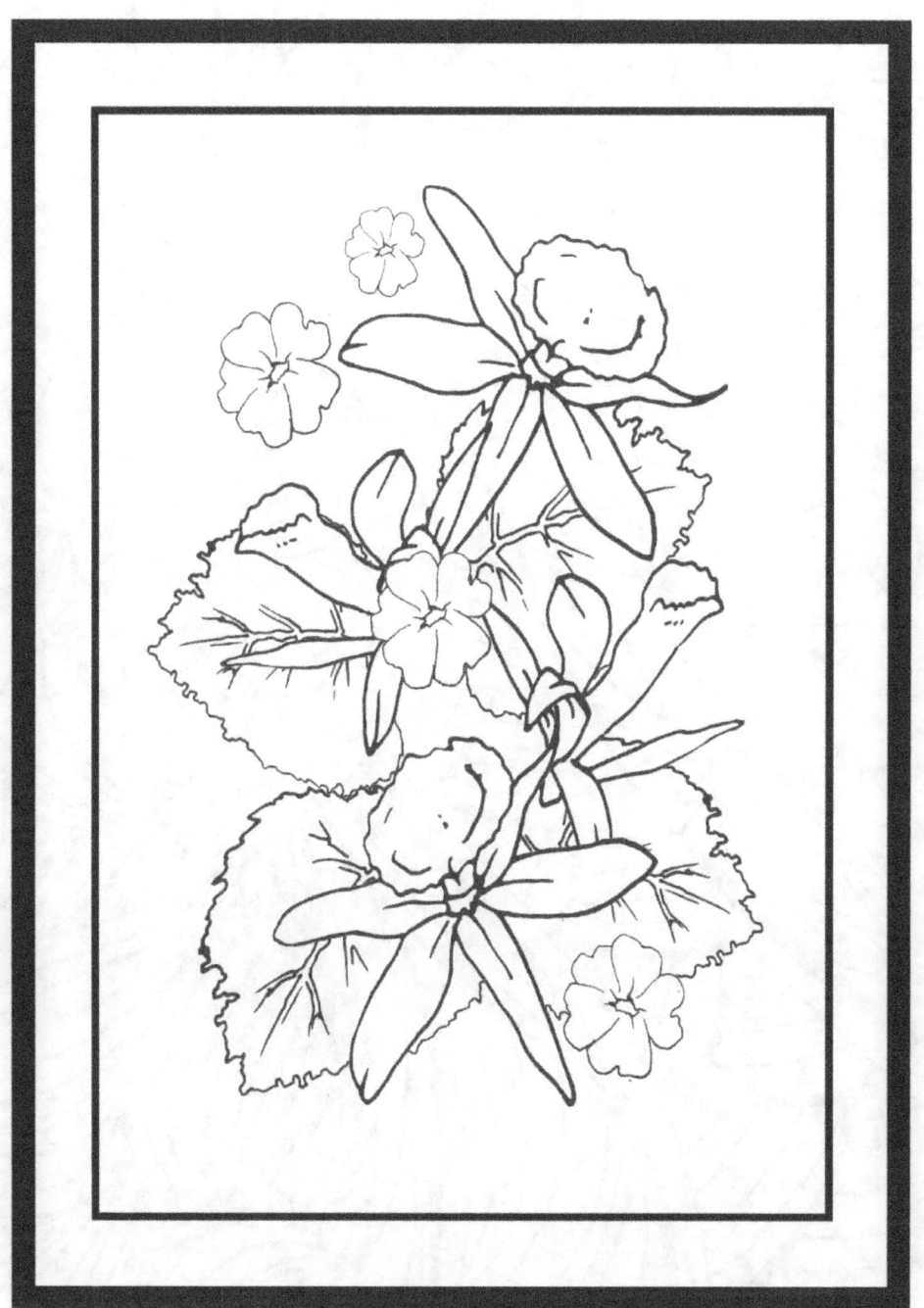

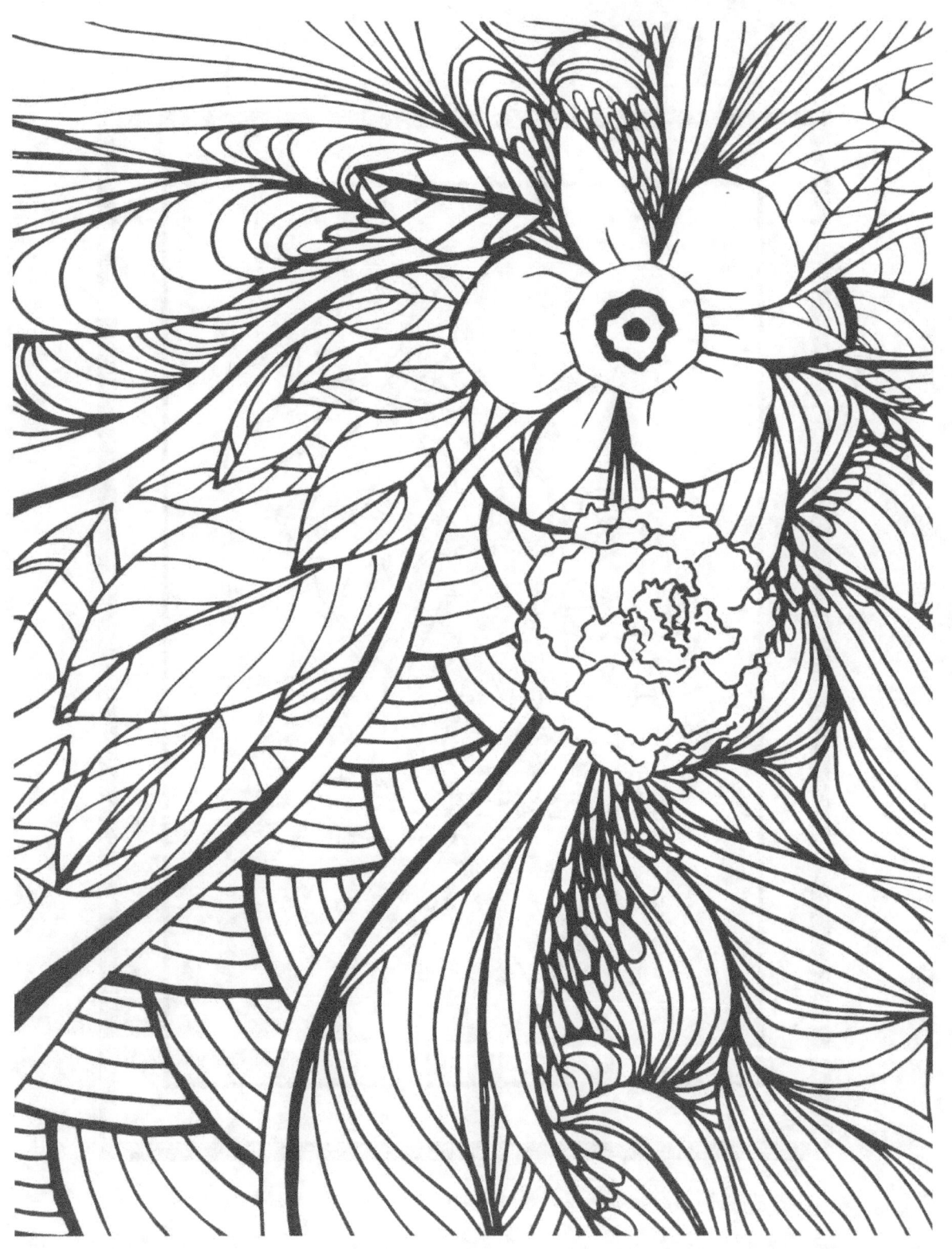

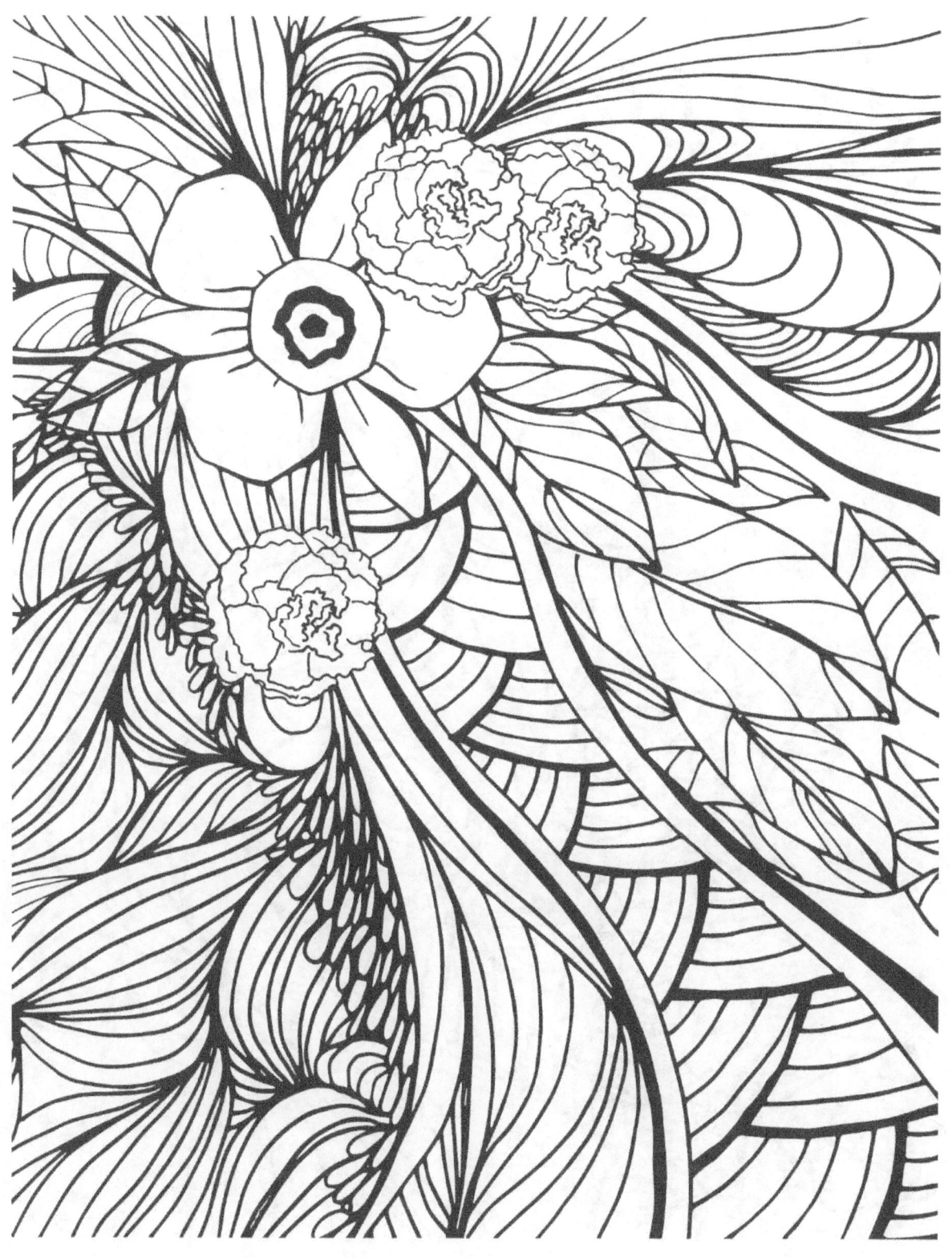

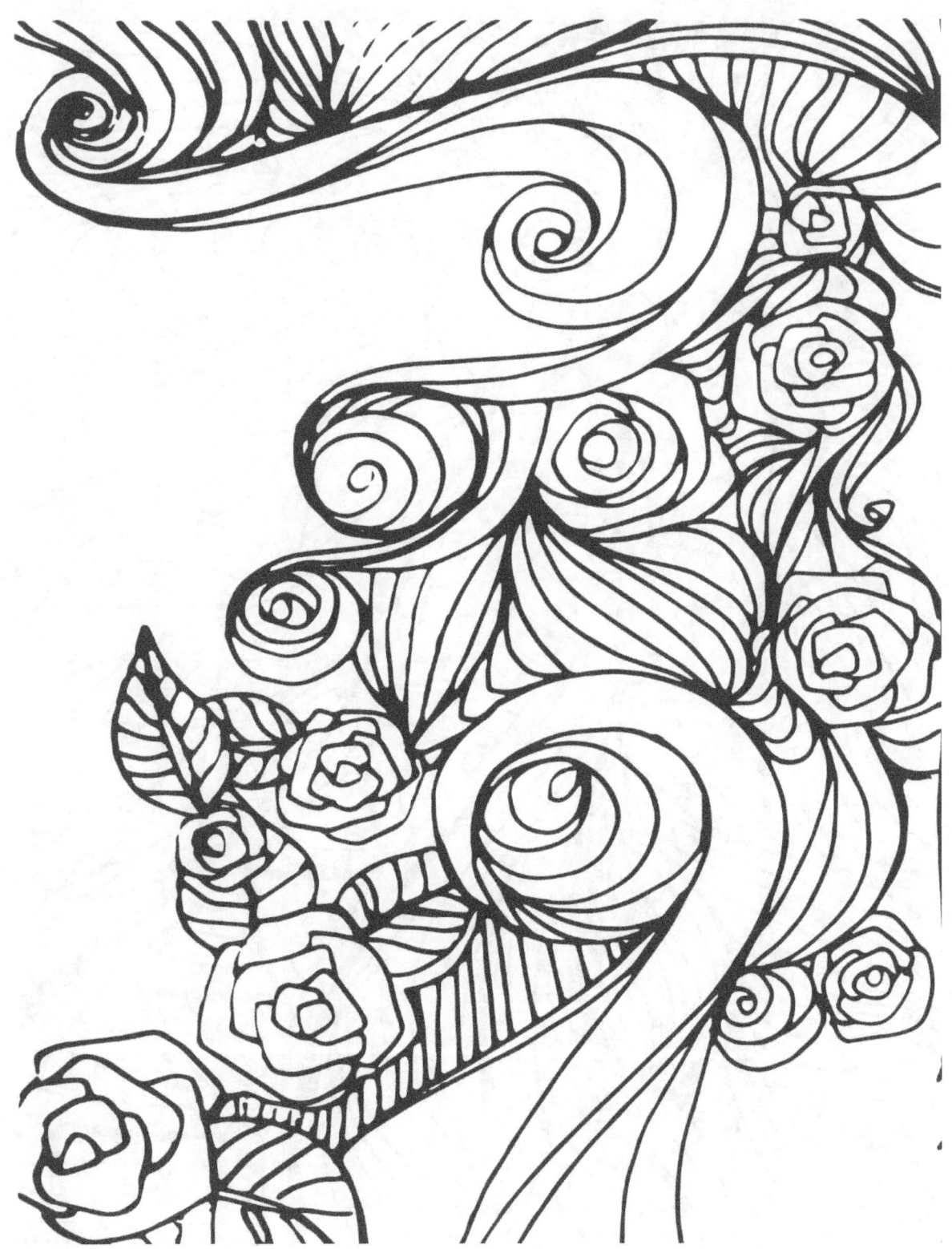

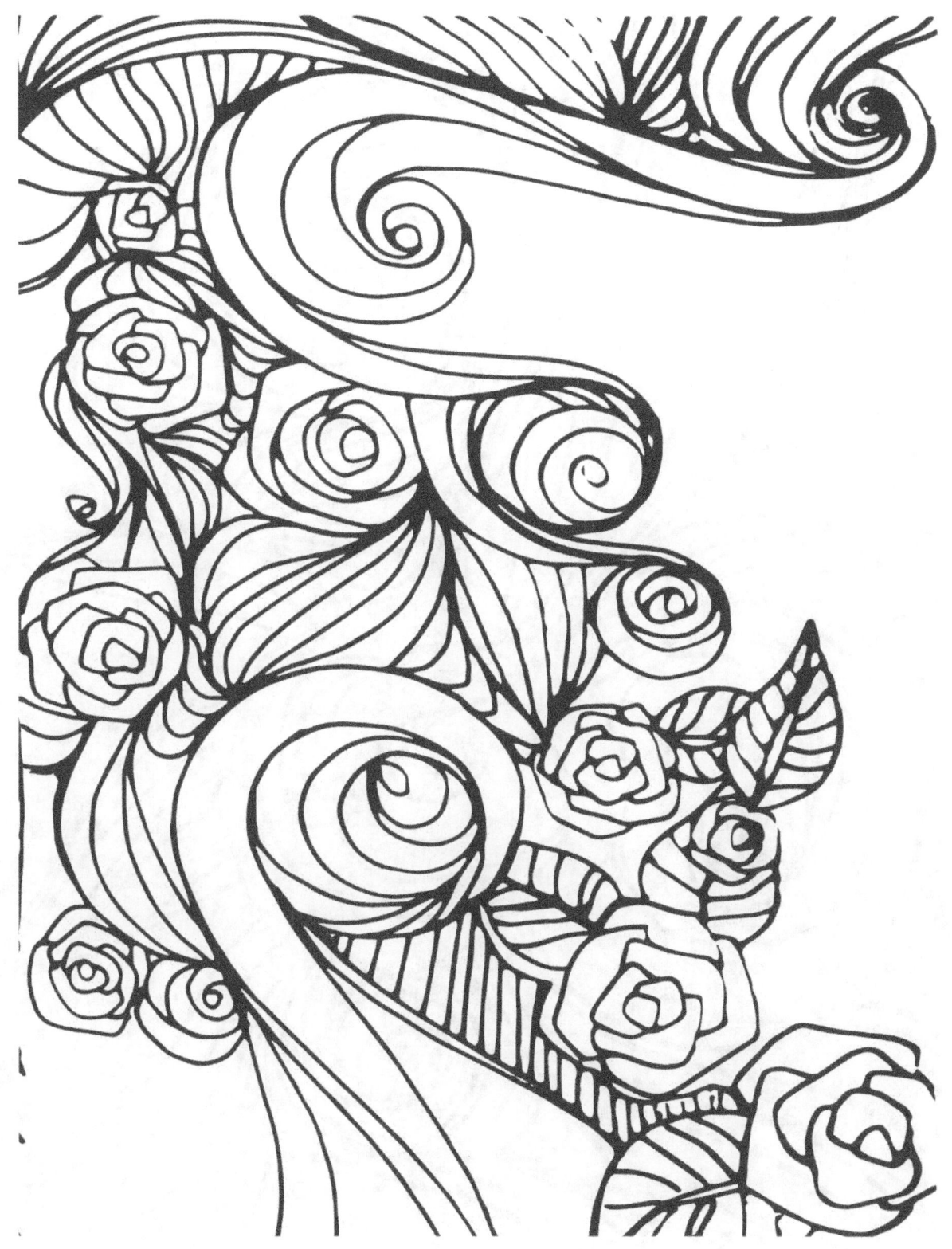

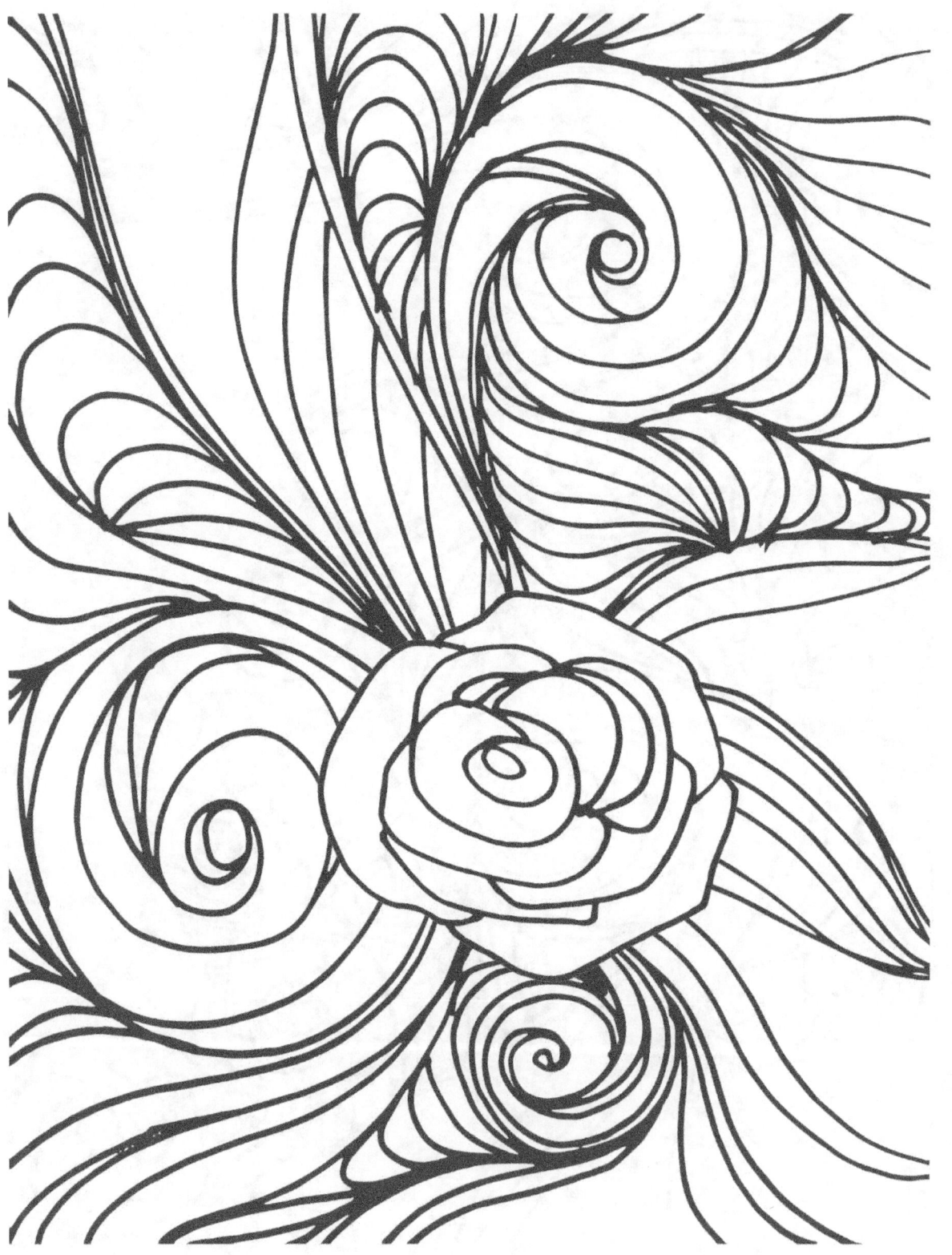

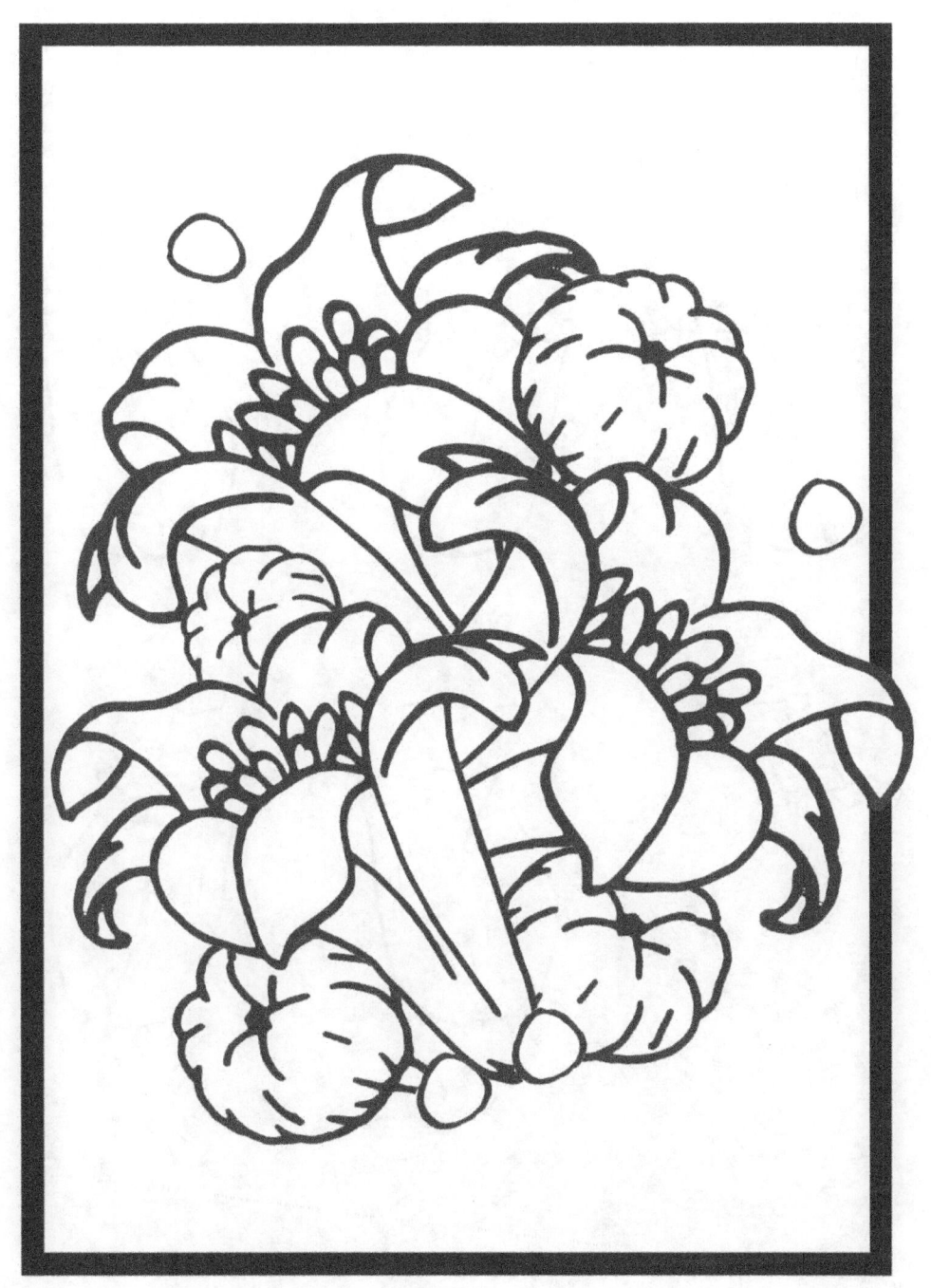

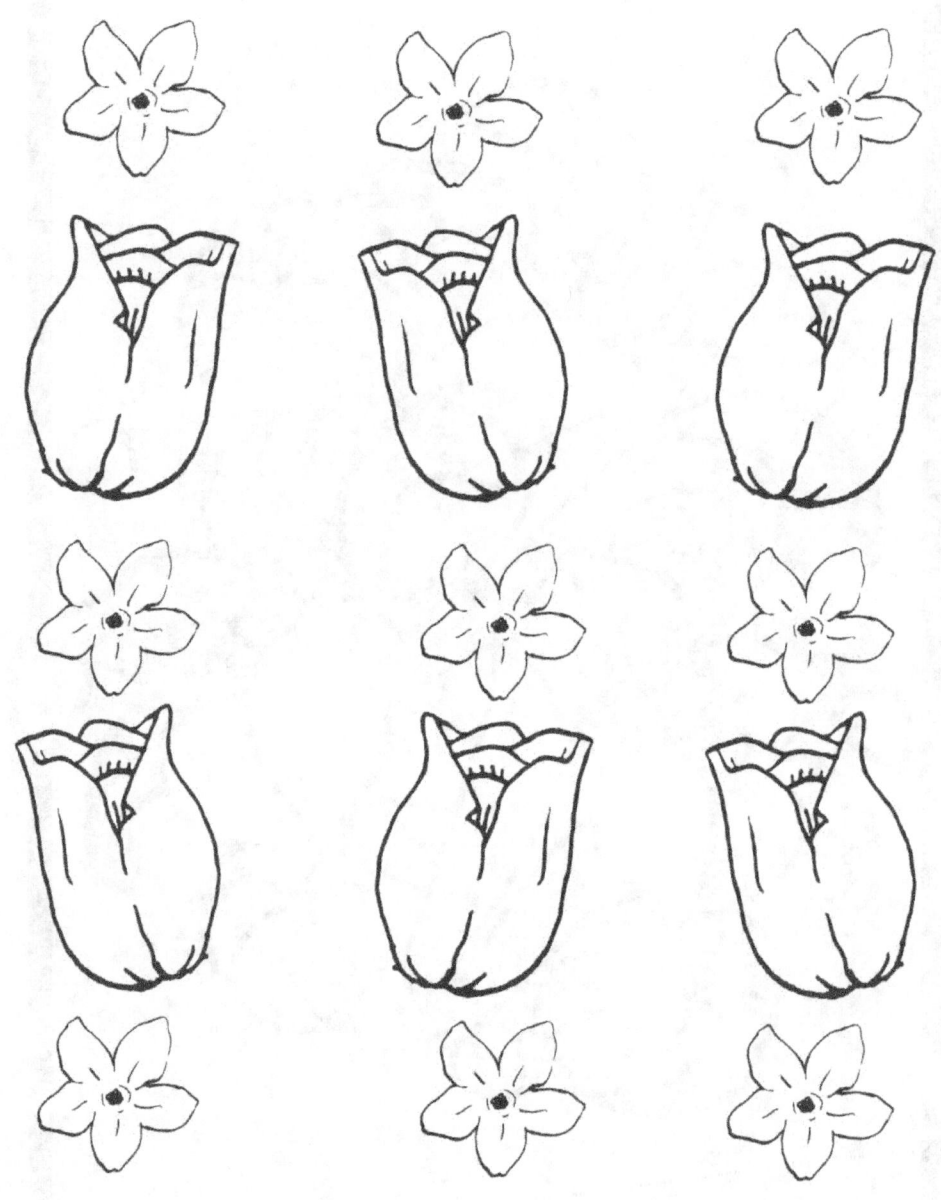

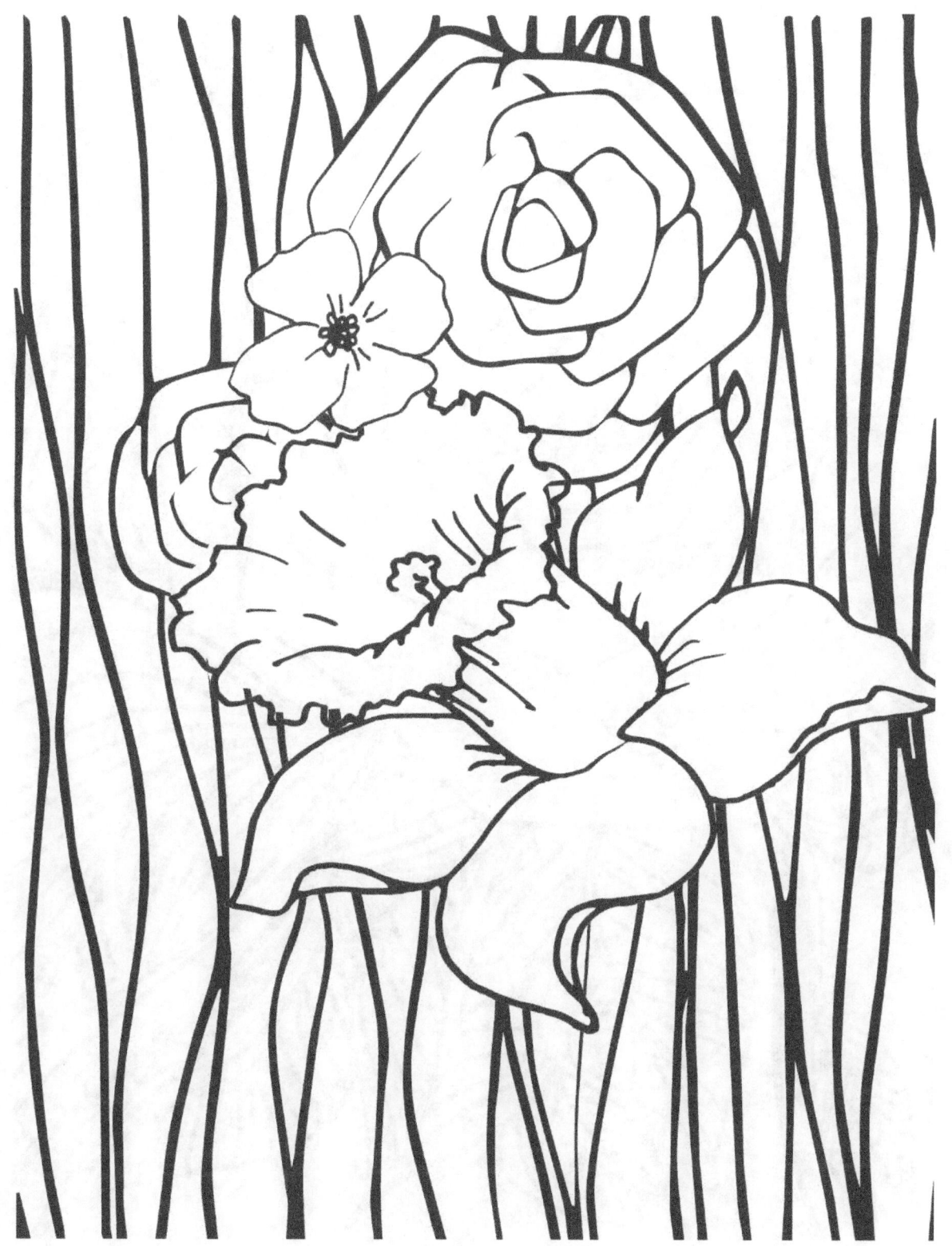

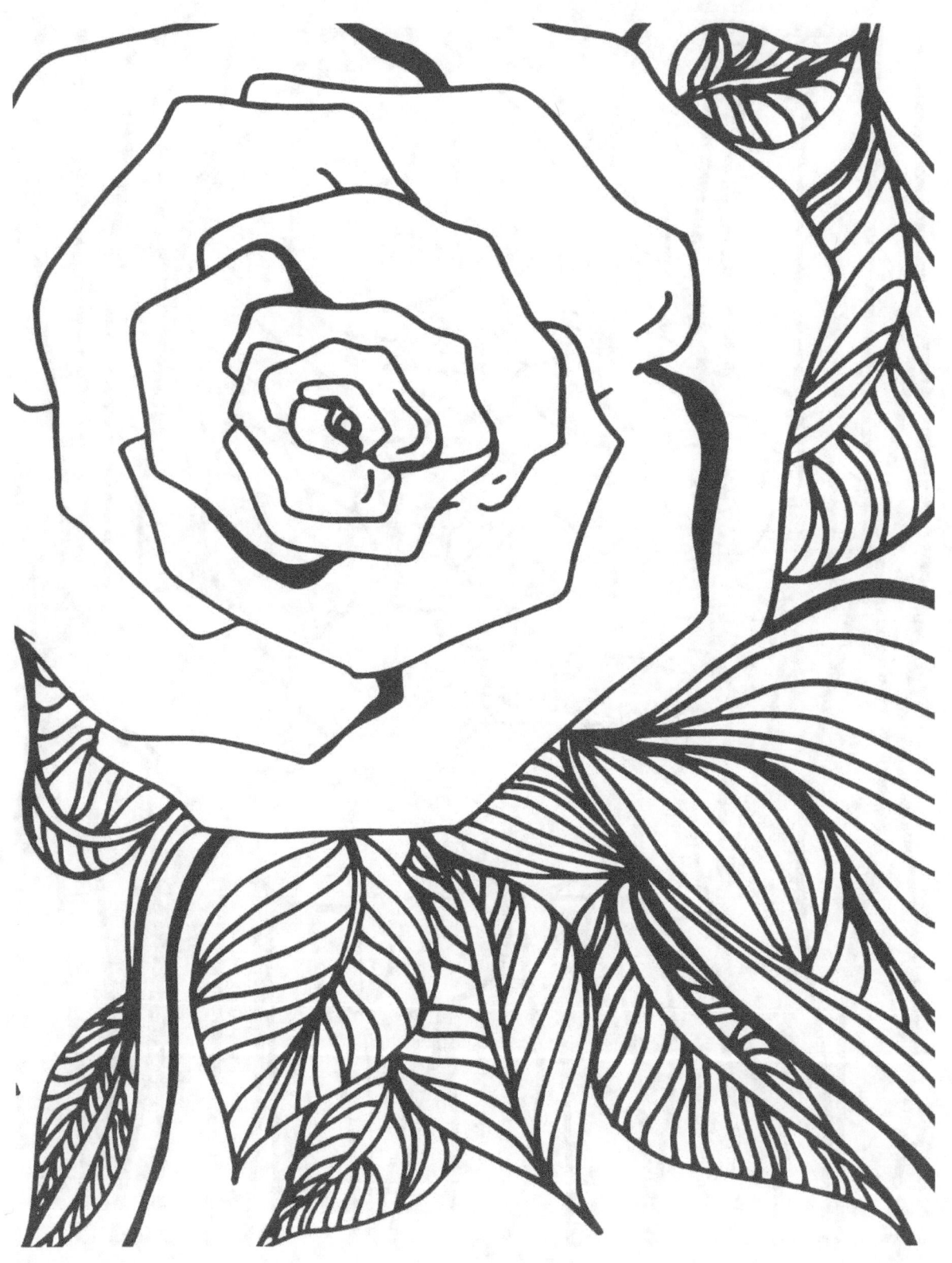

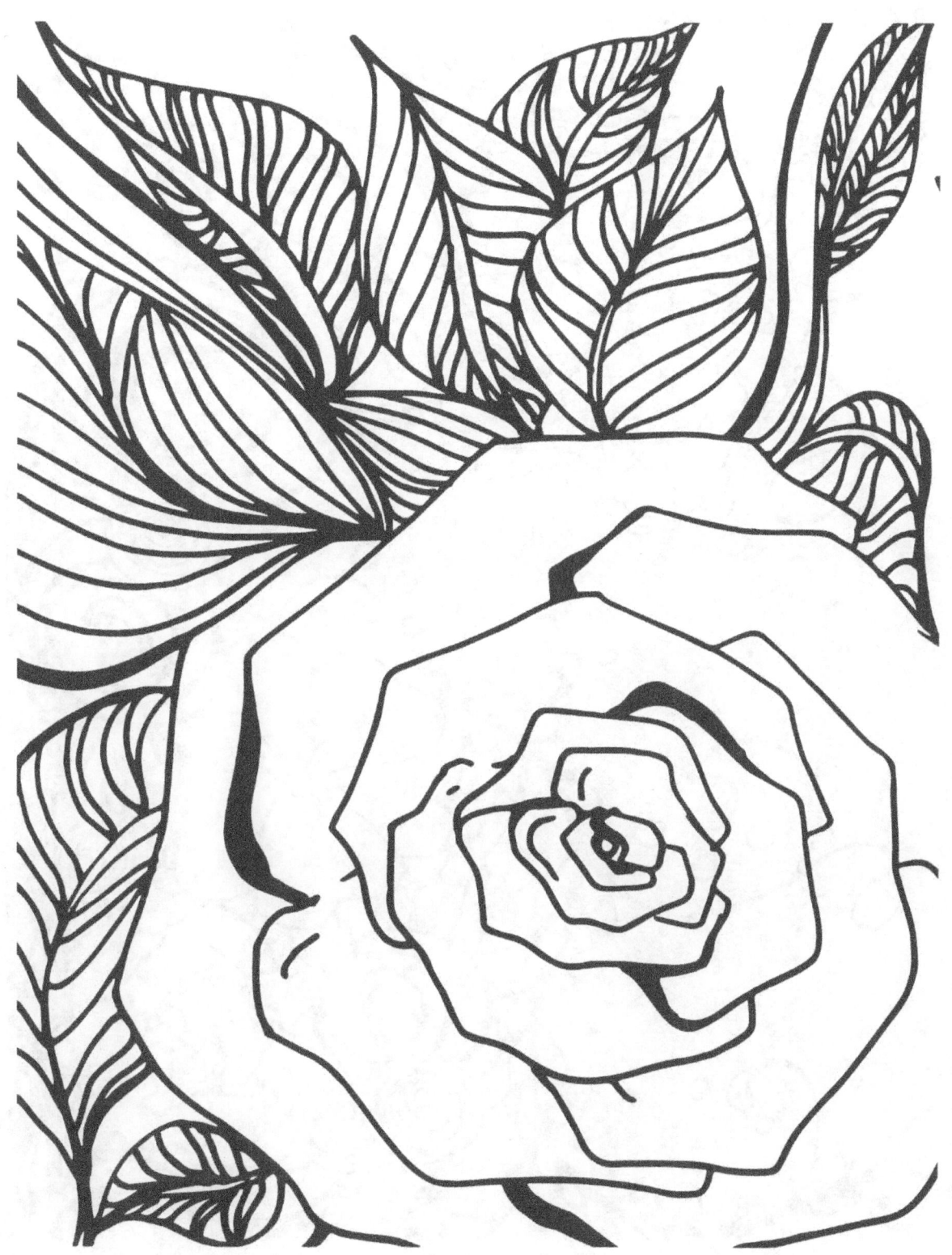

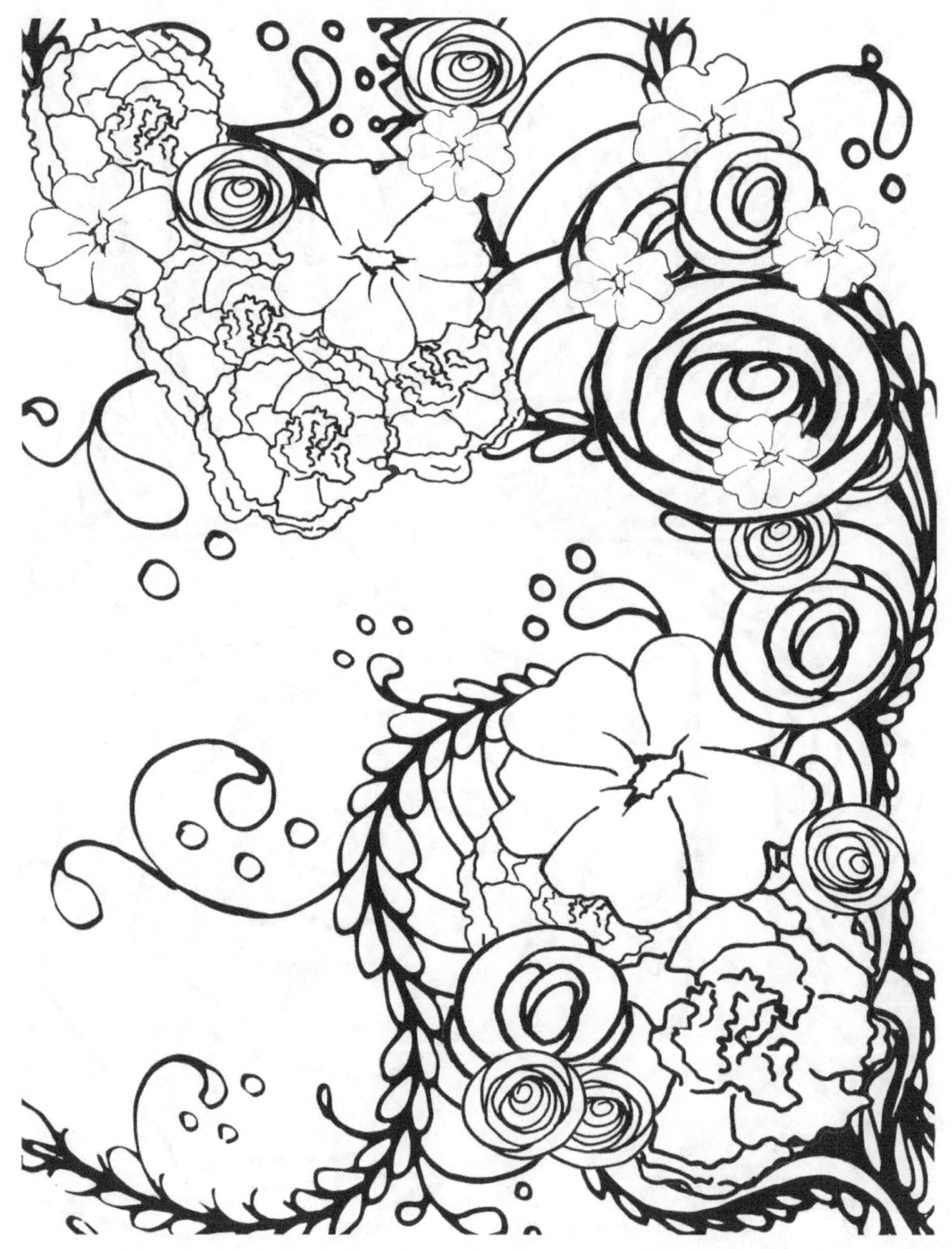

84

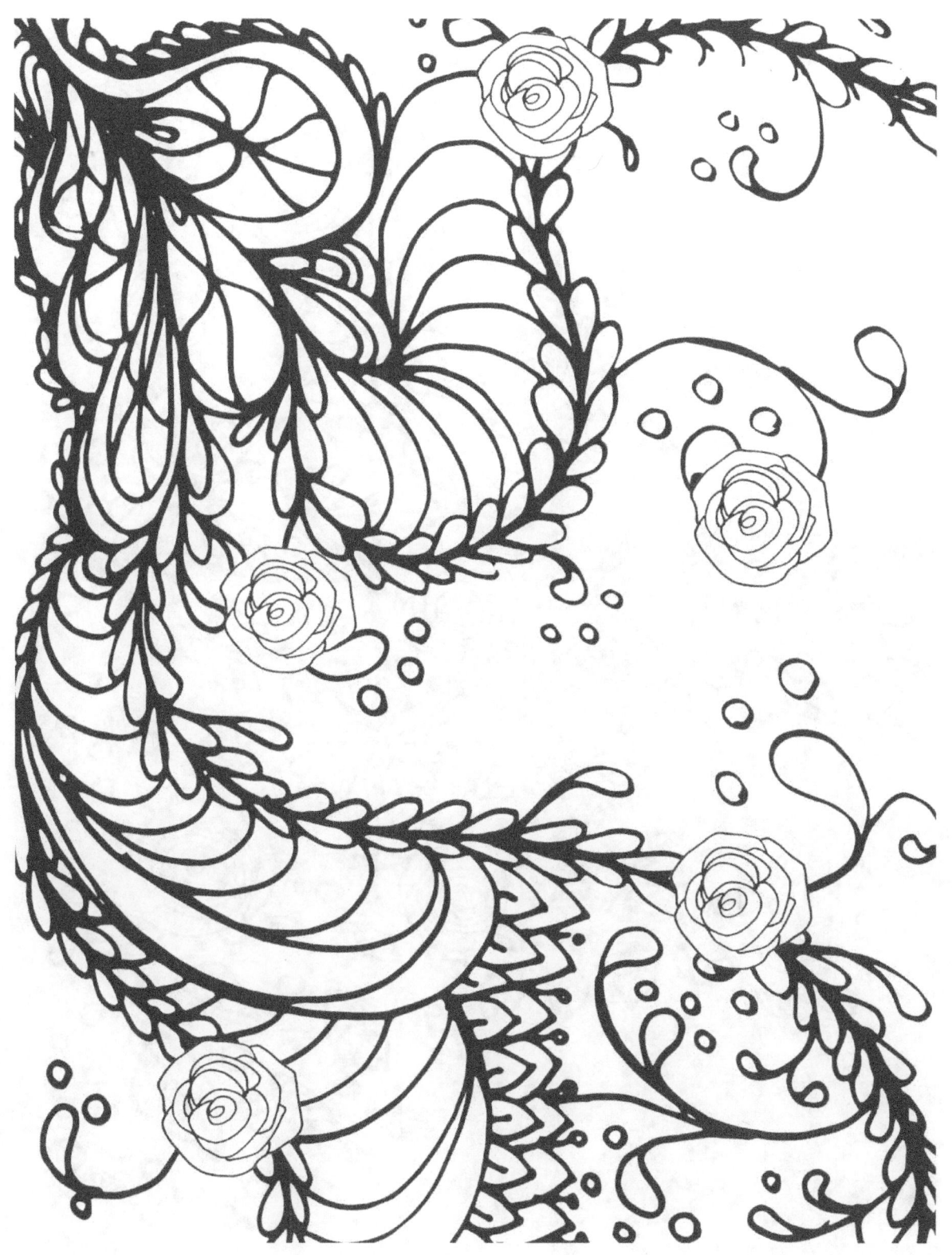

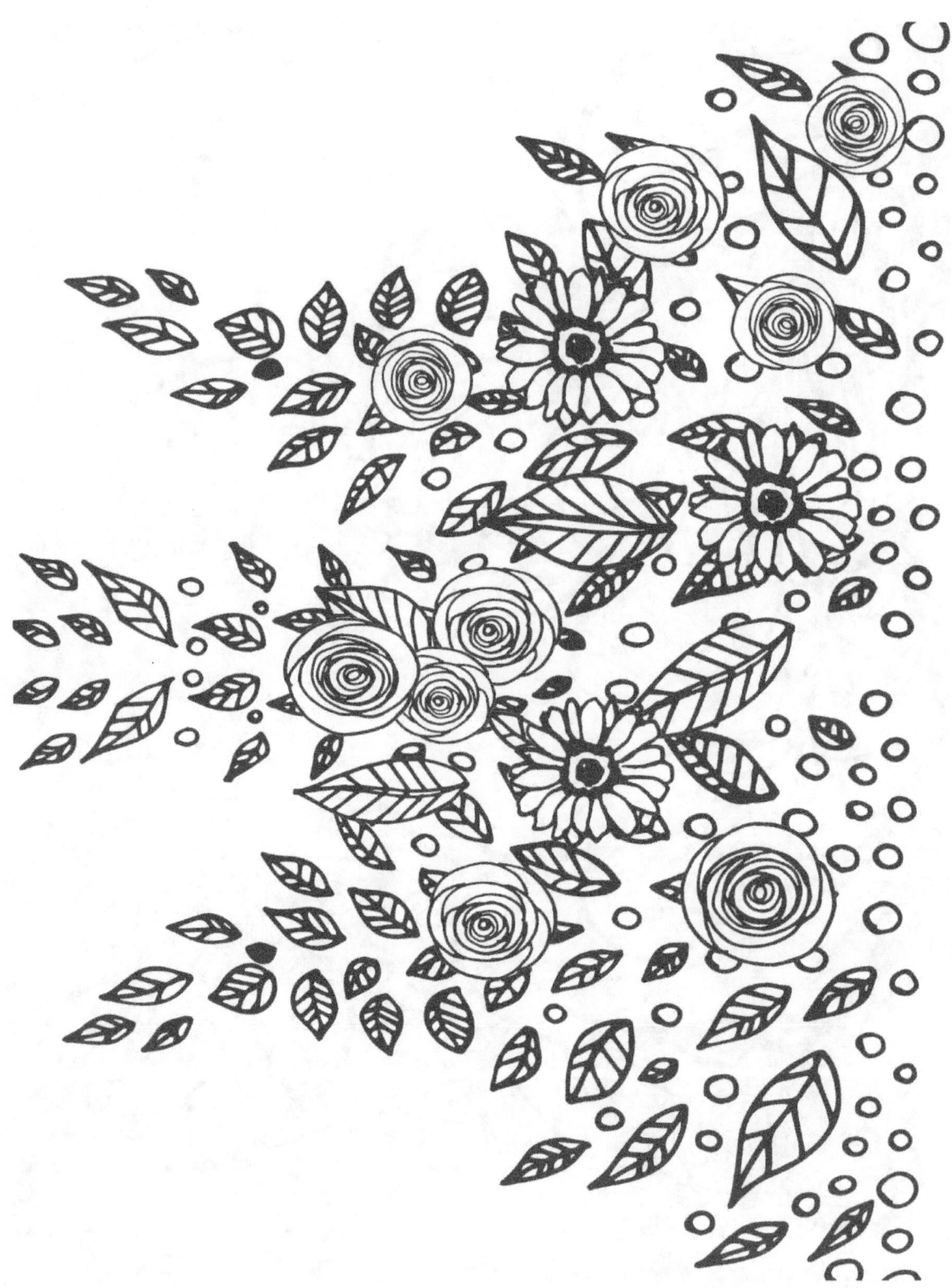

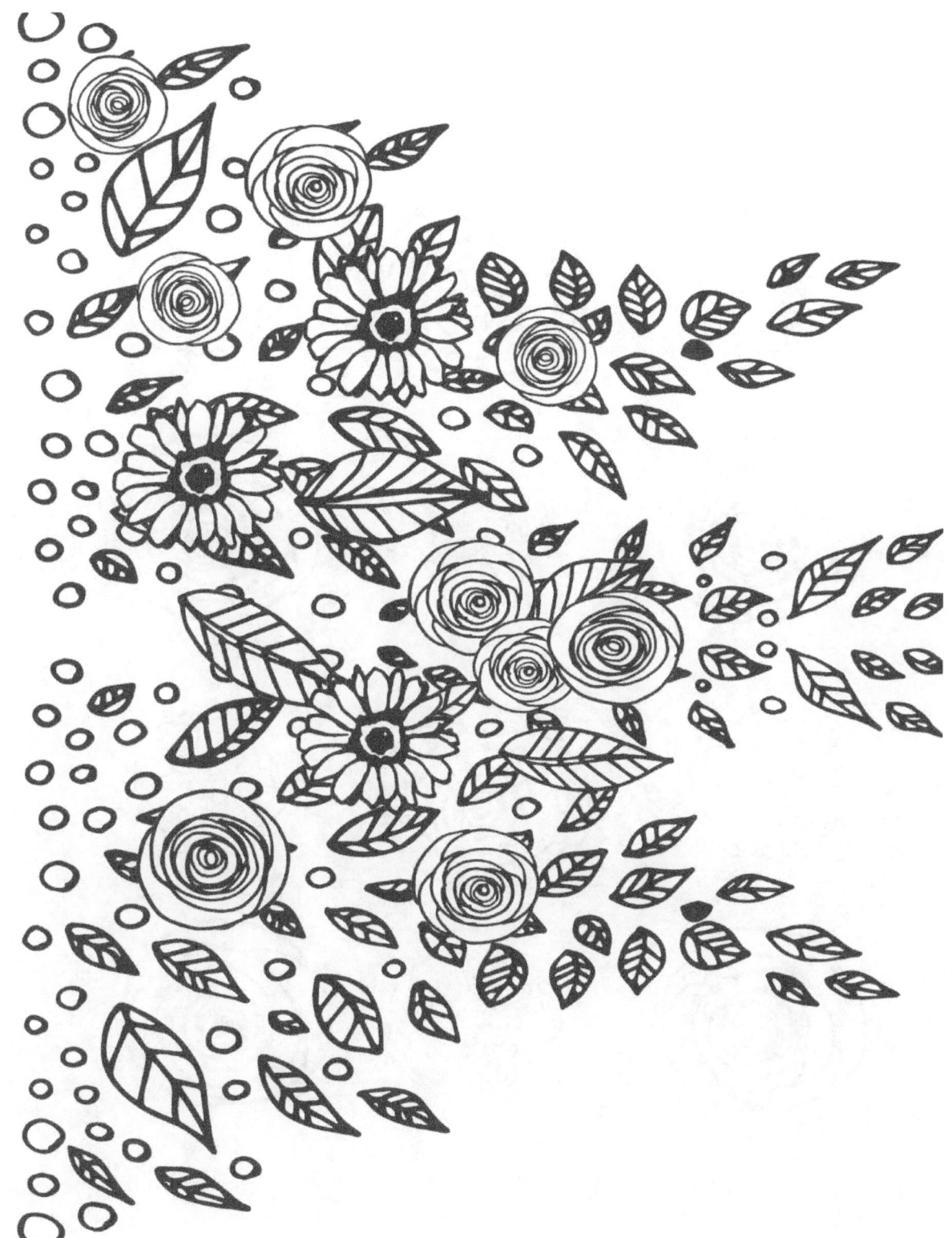

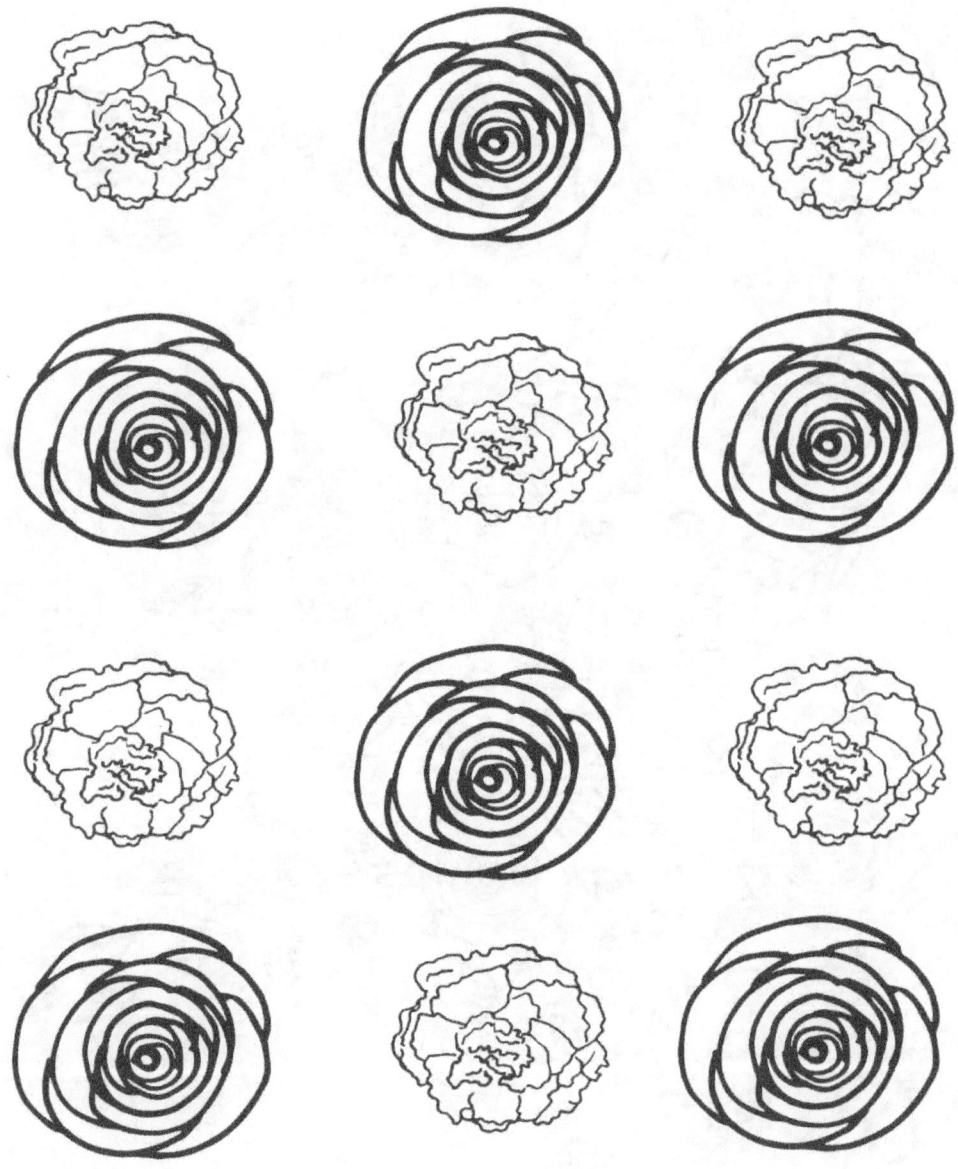

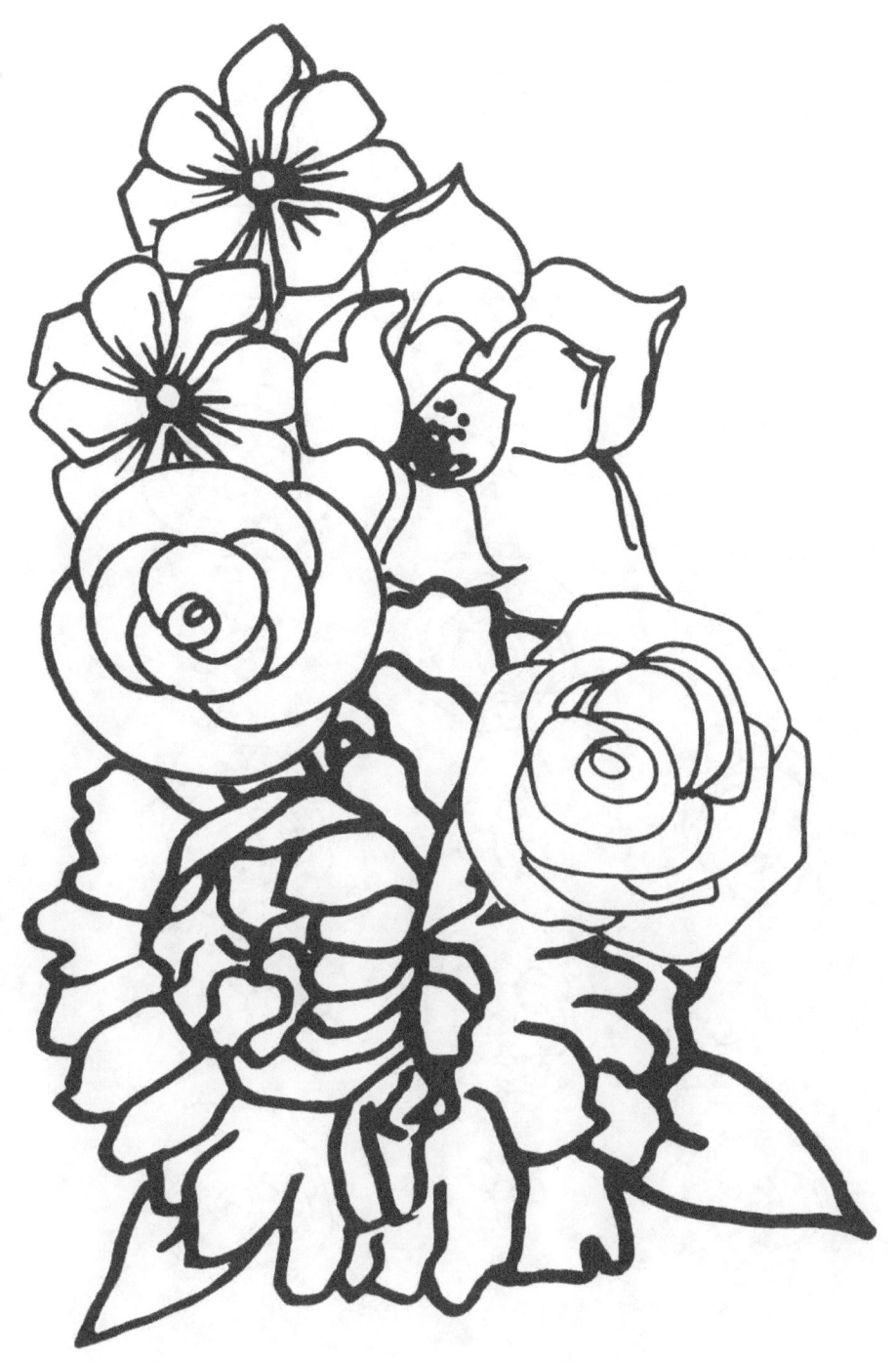

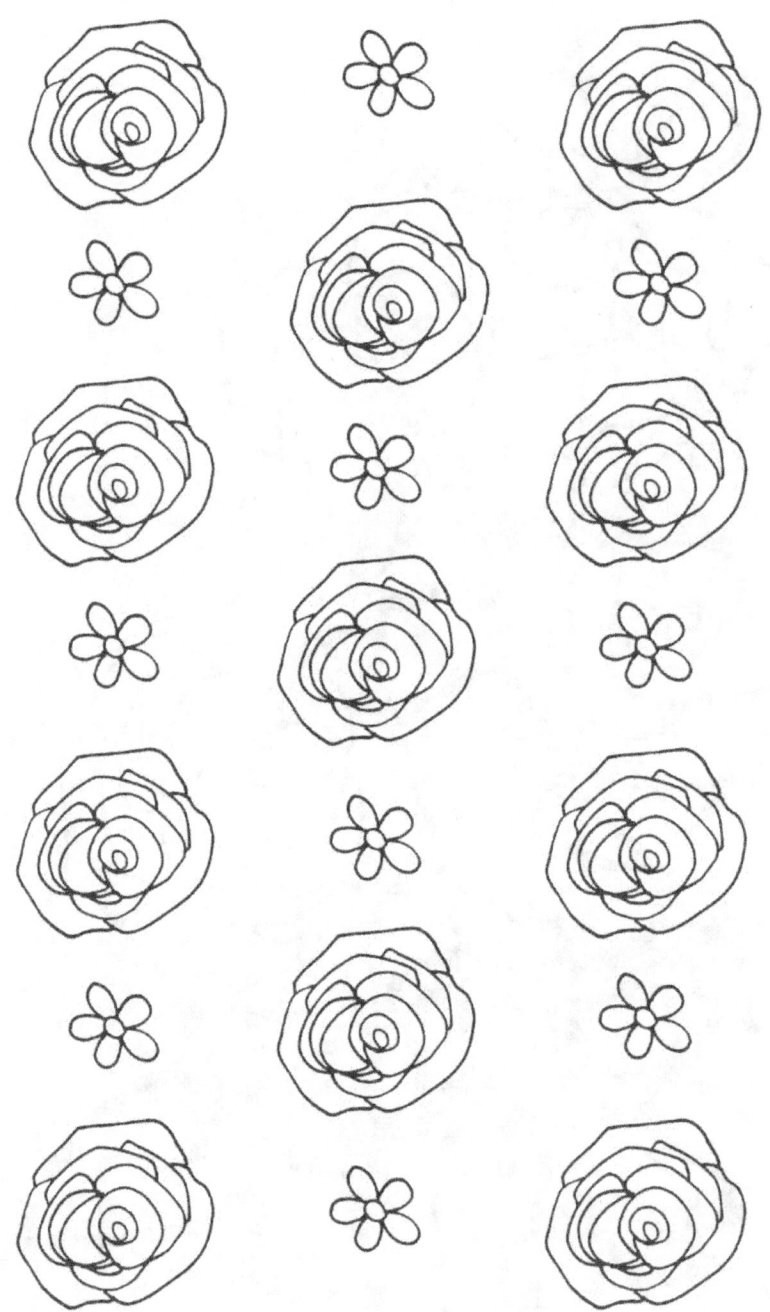

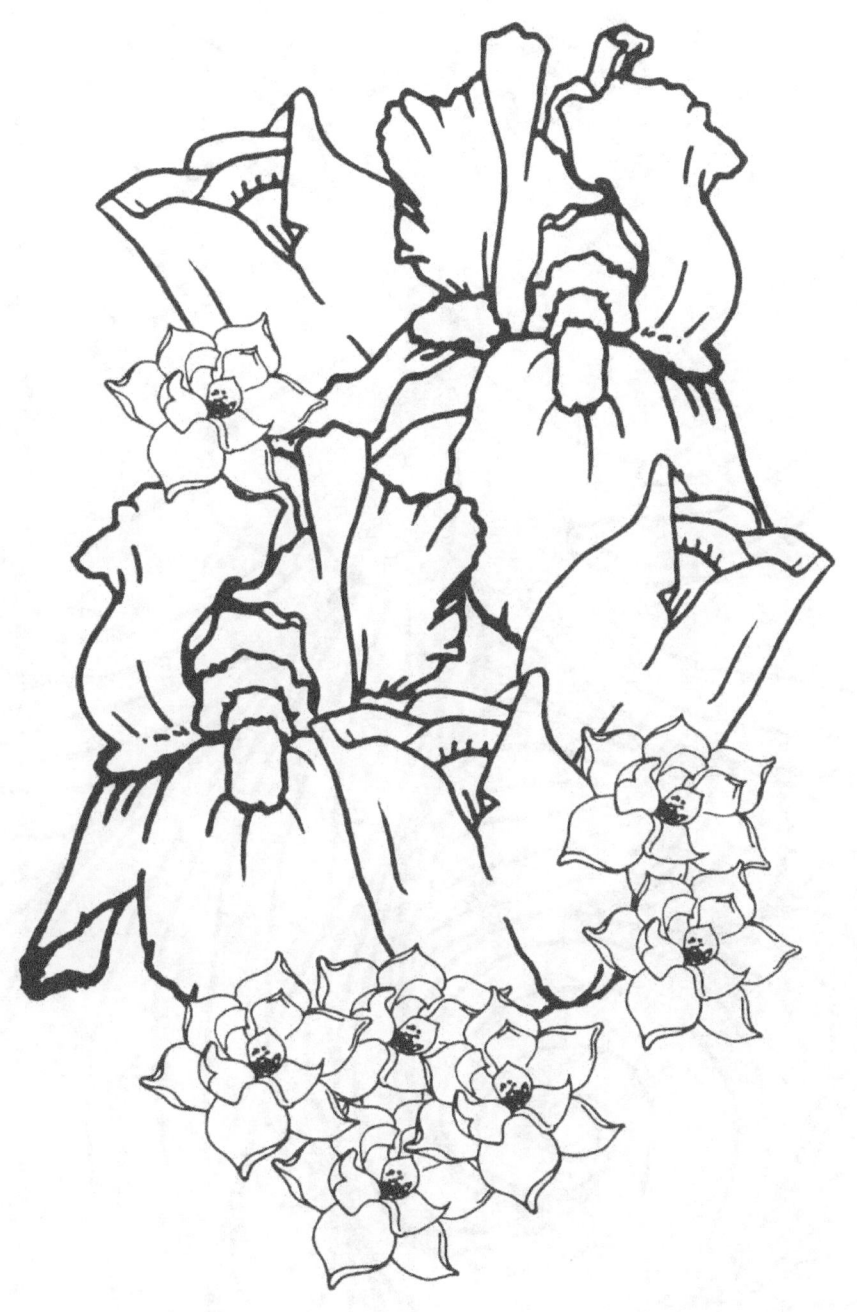

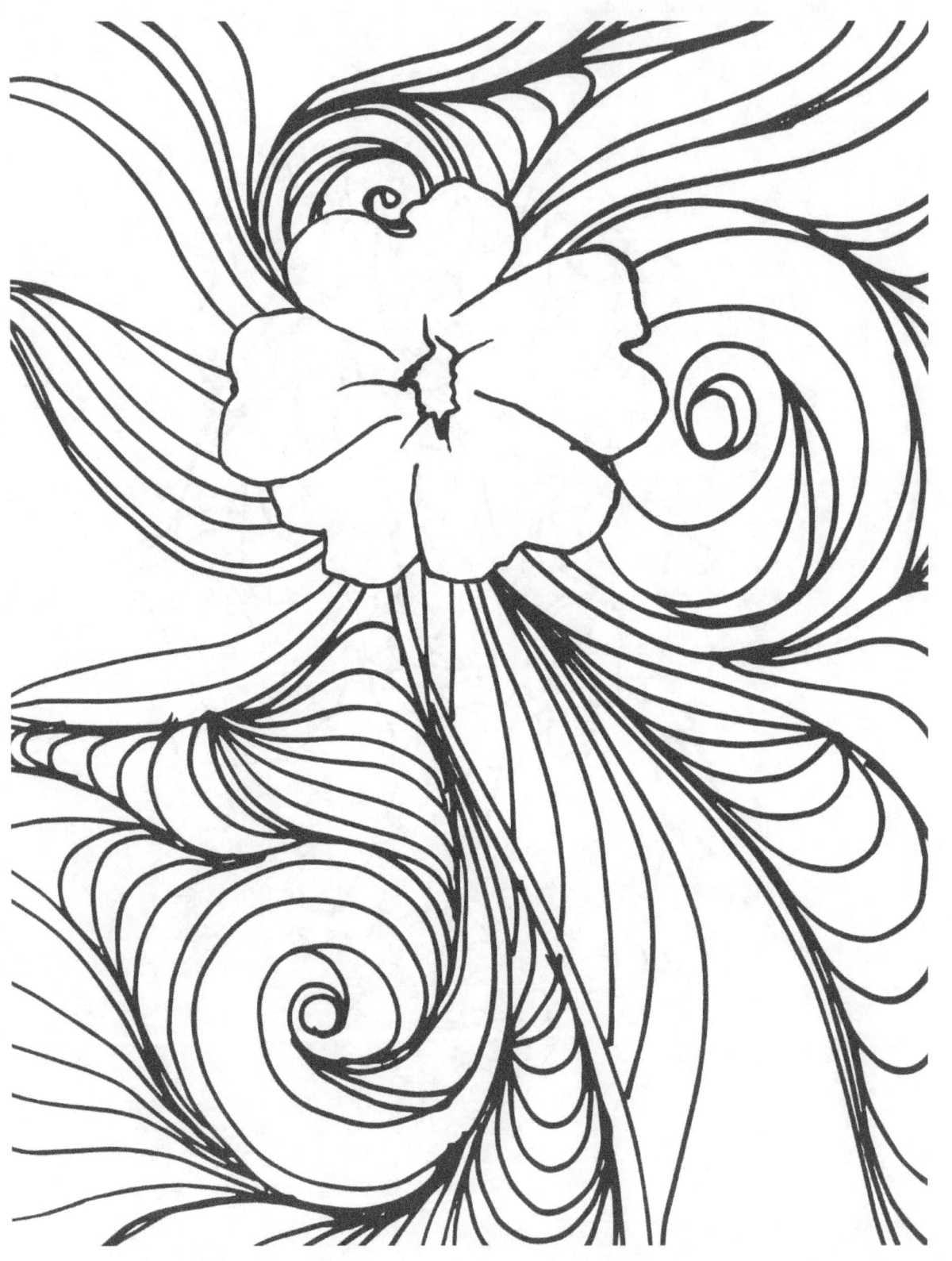

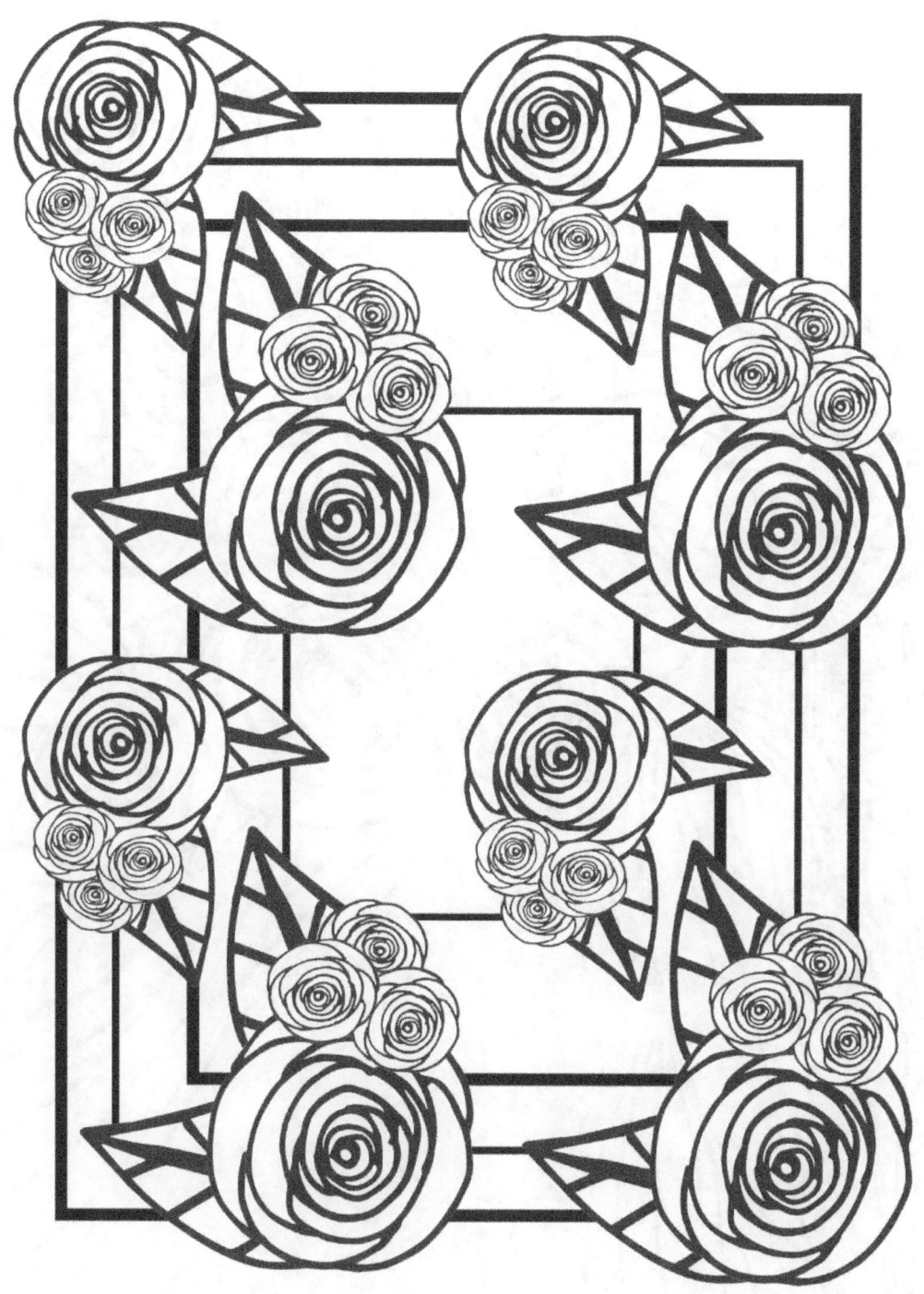

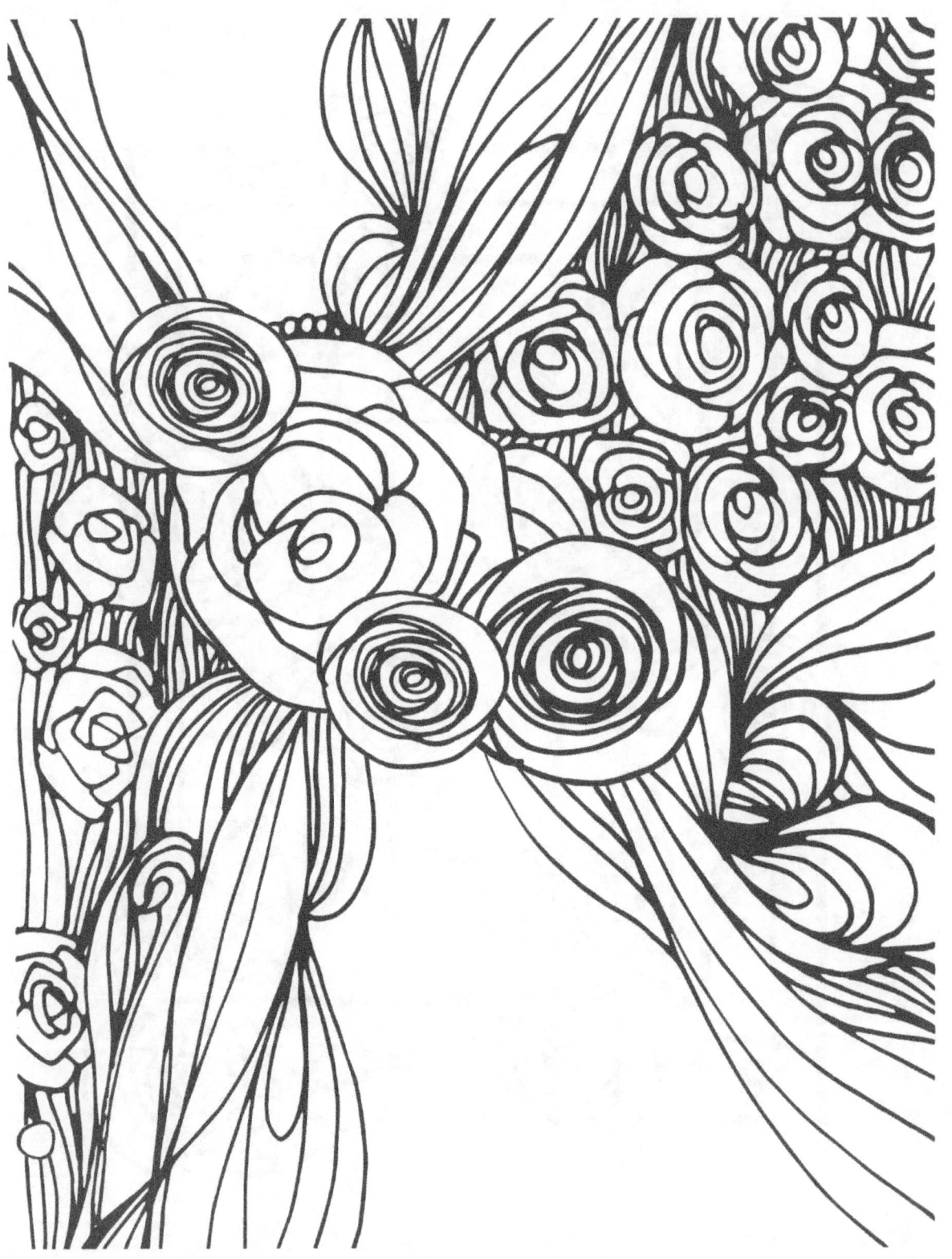

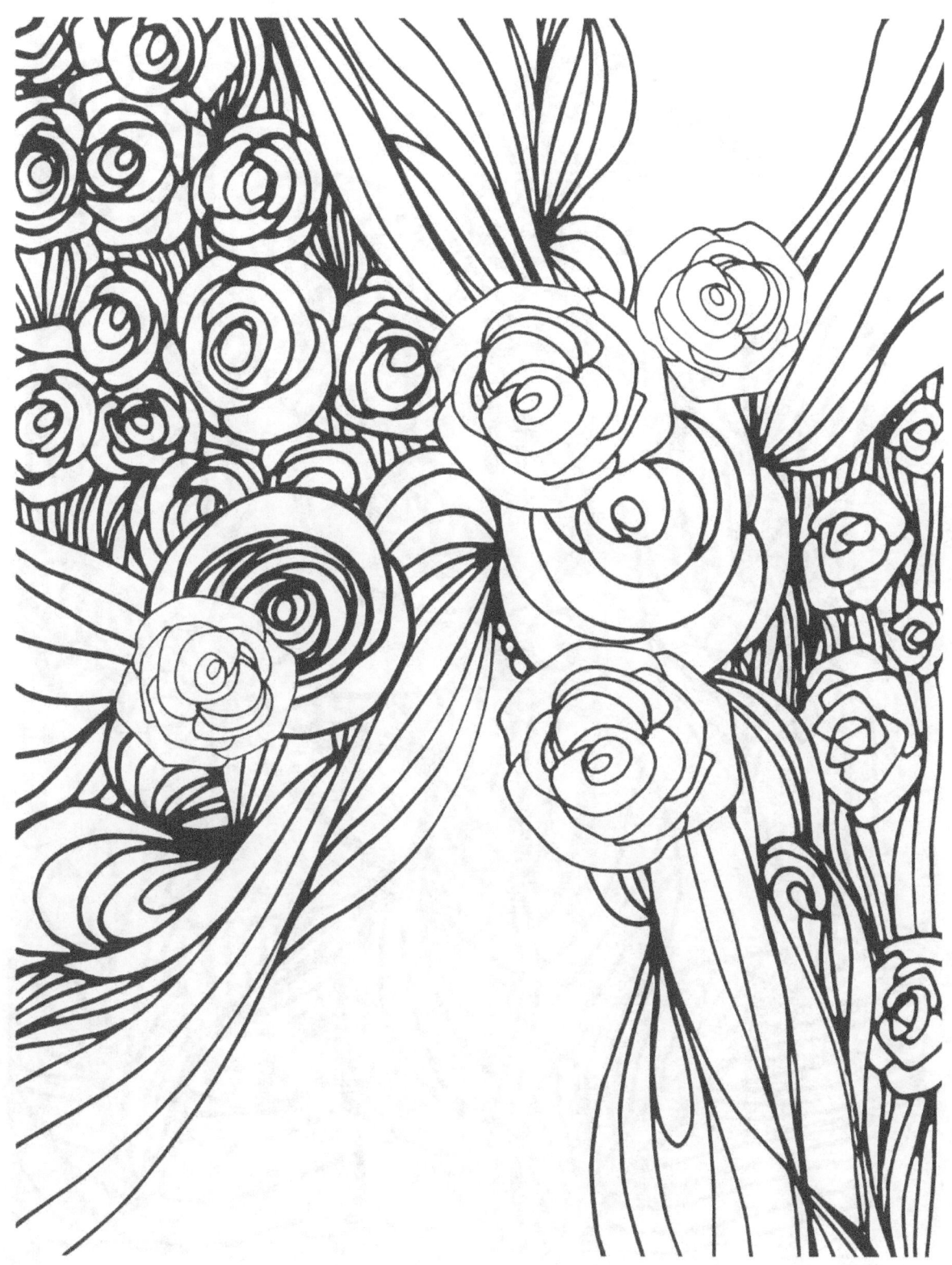

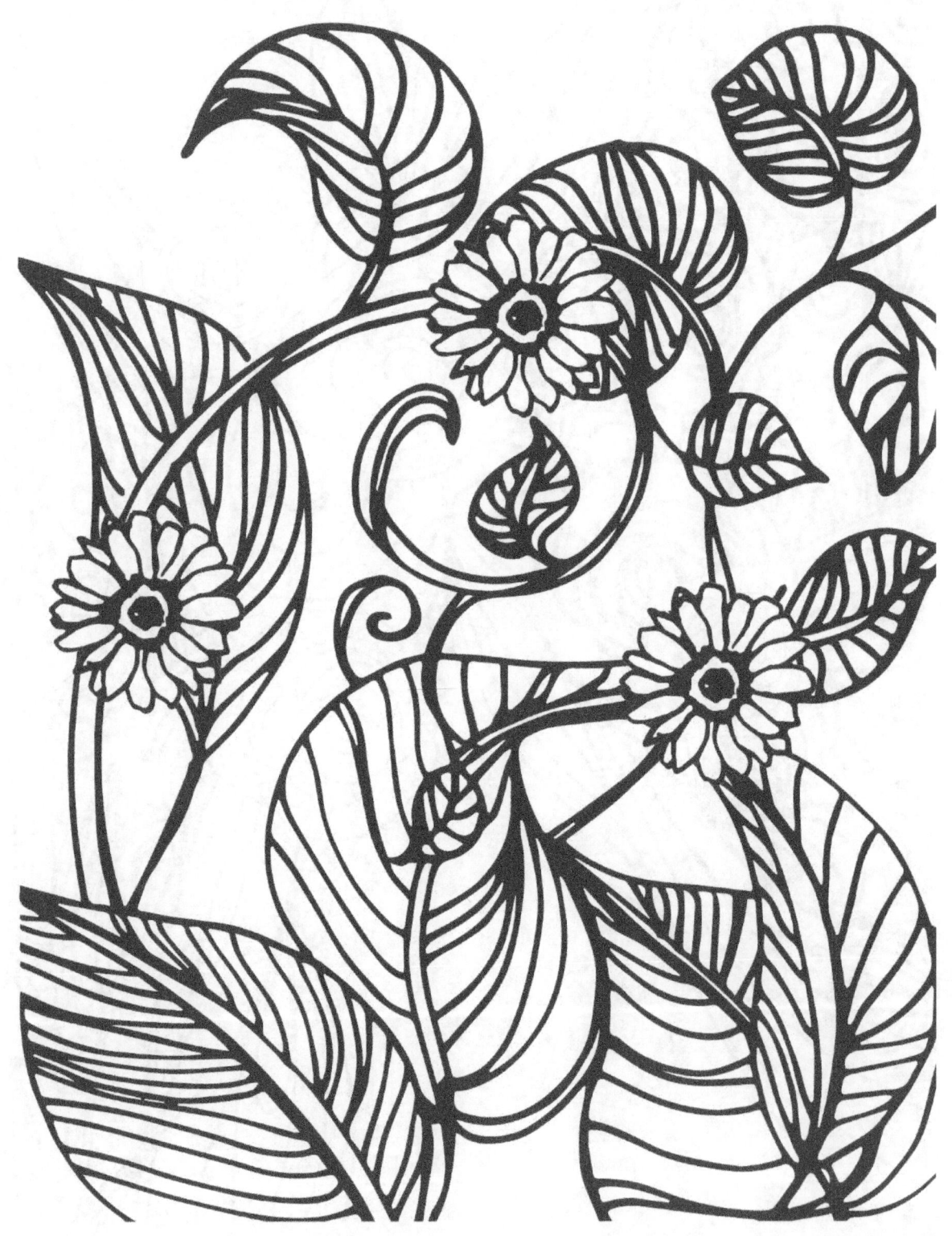

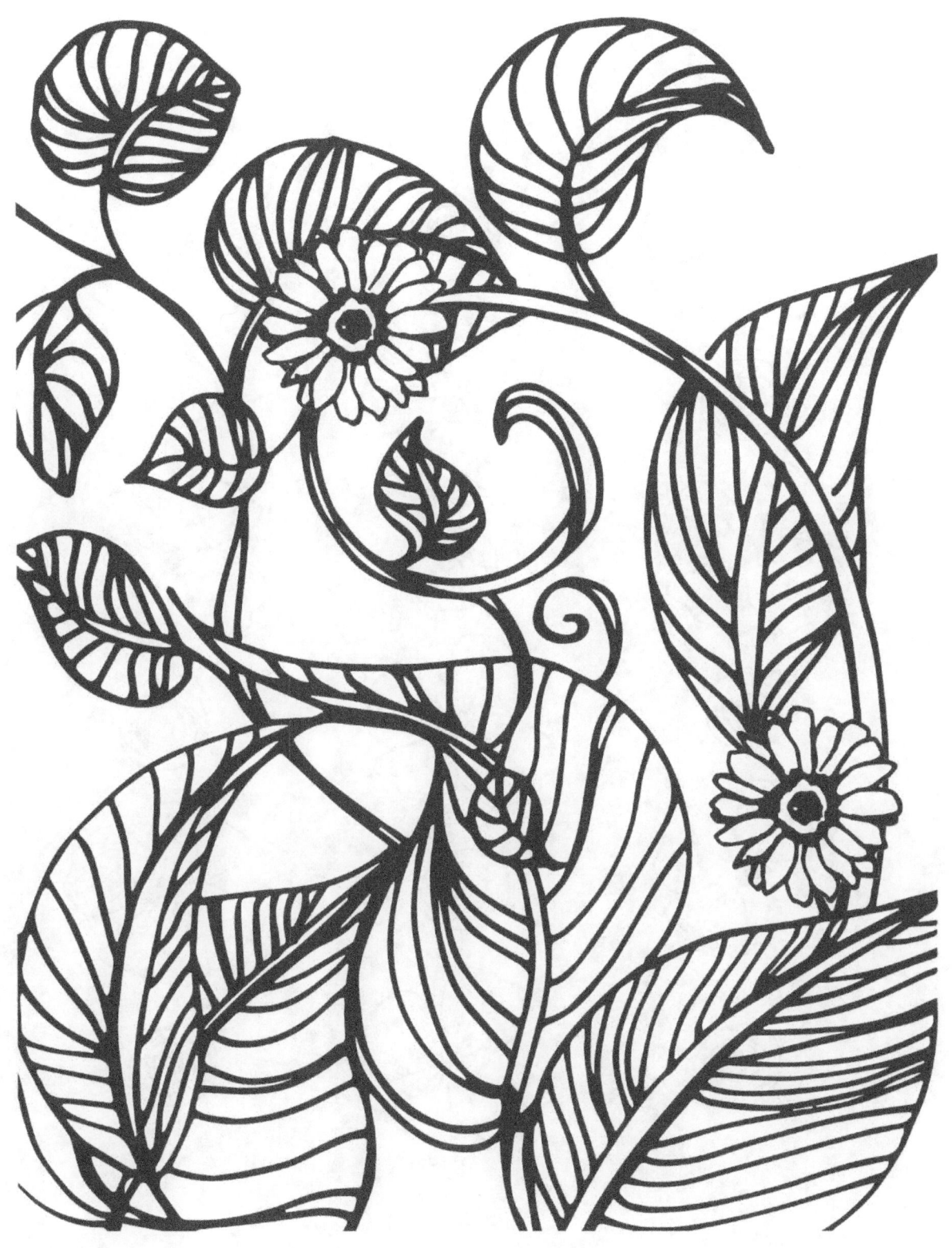

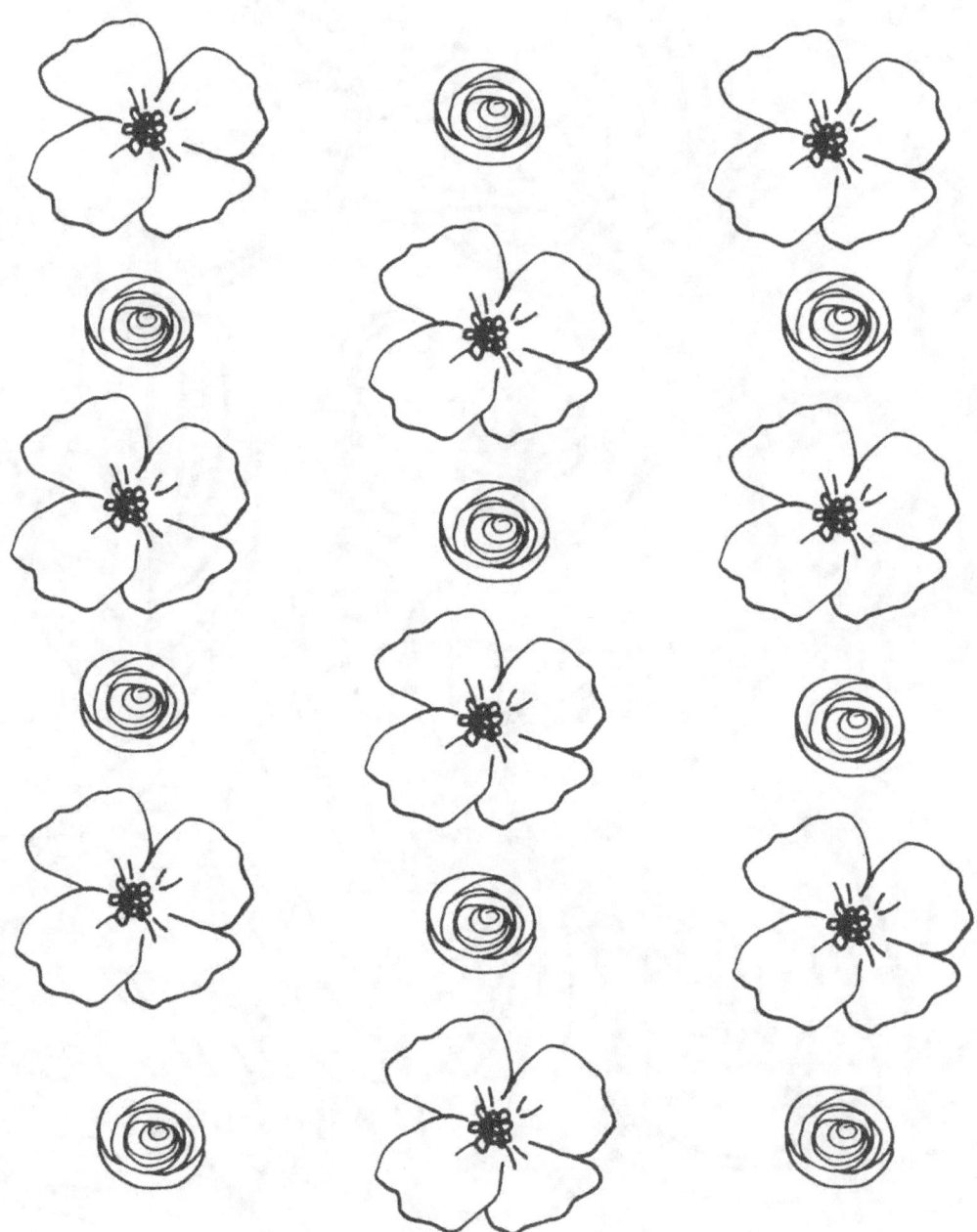

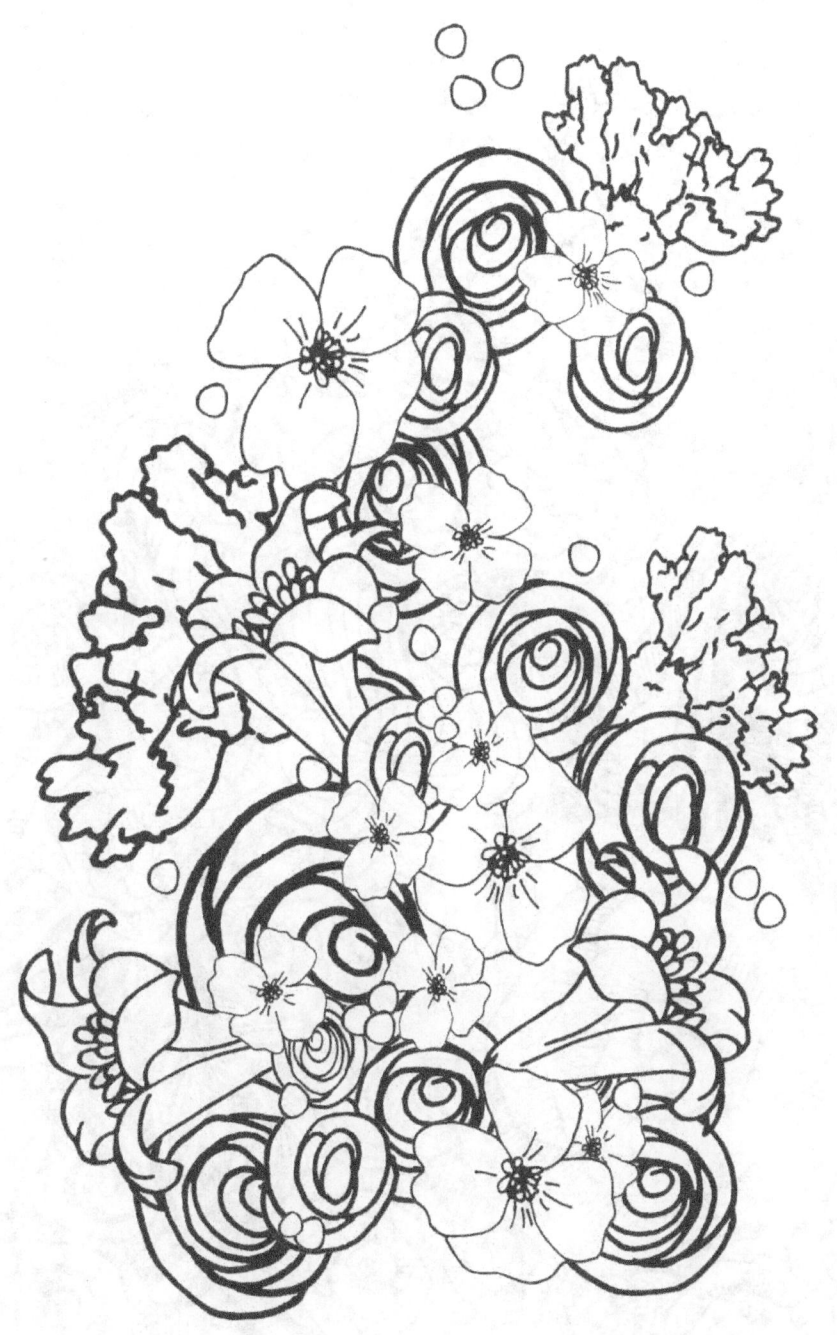

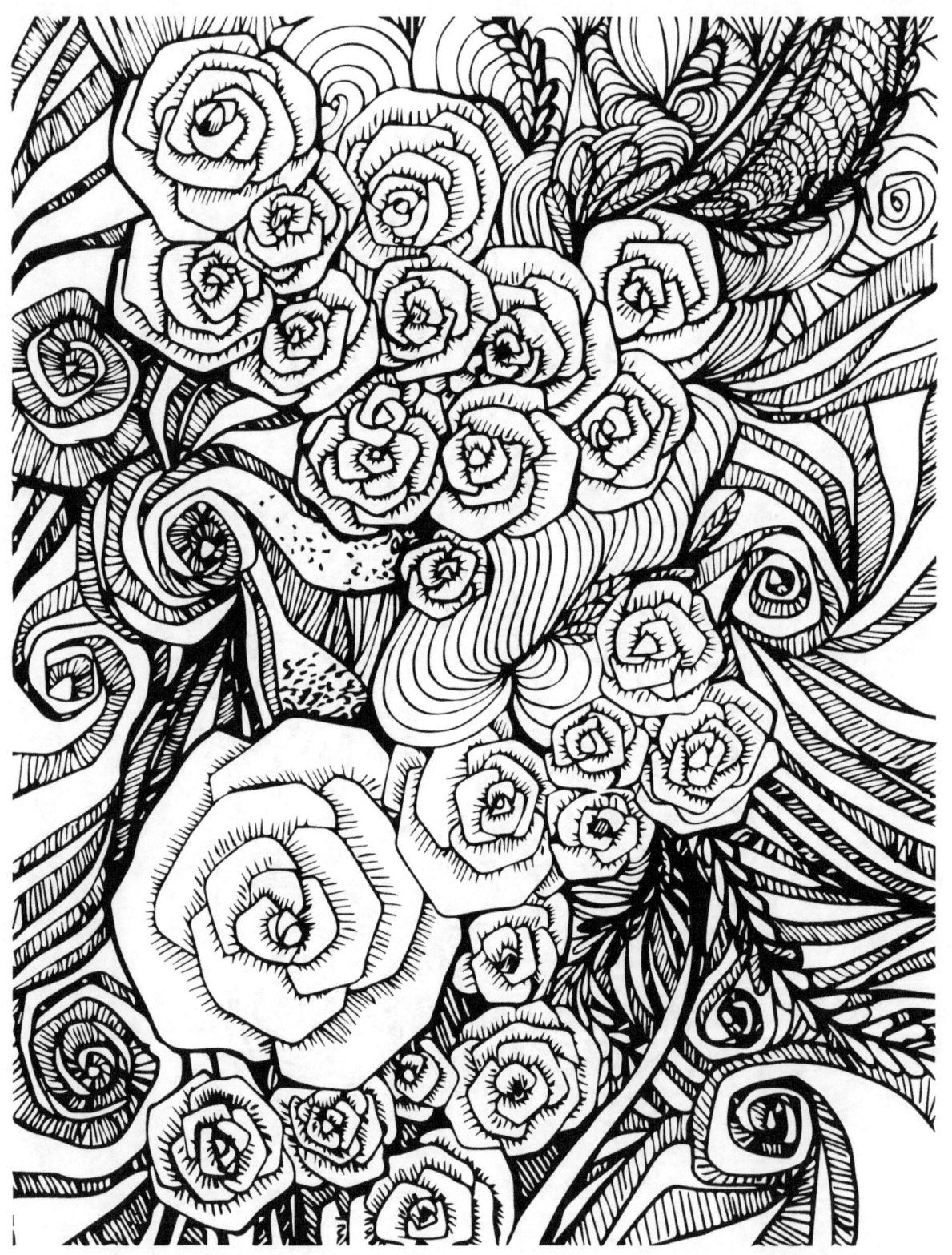

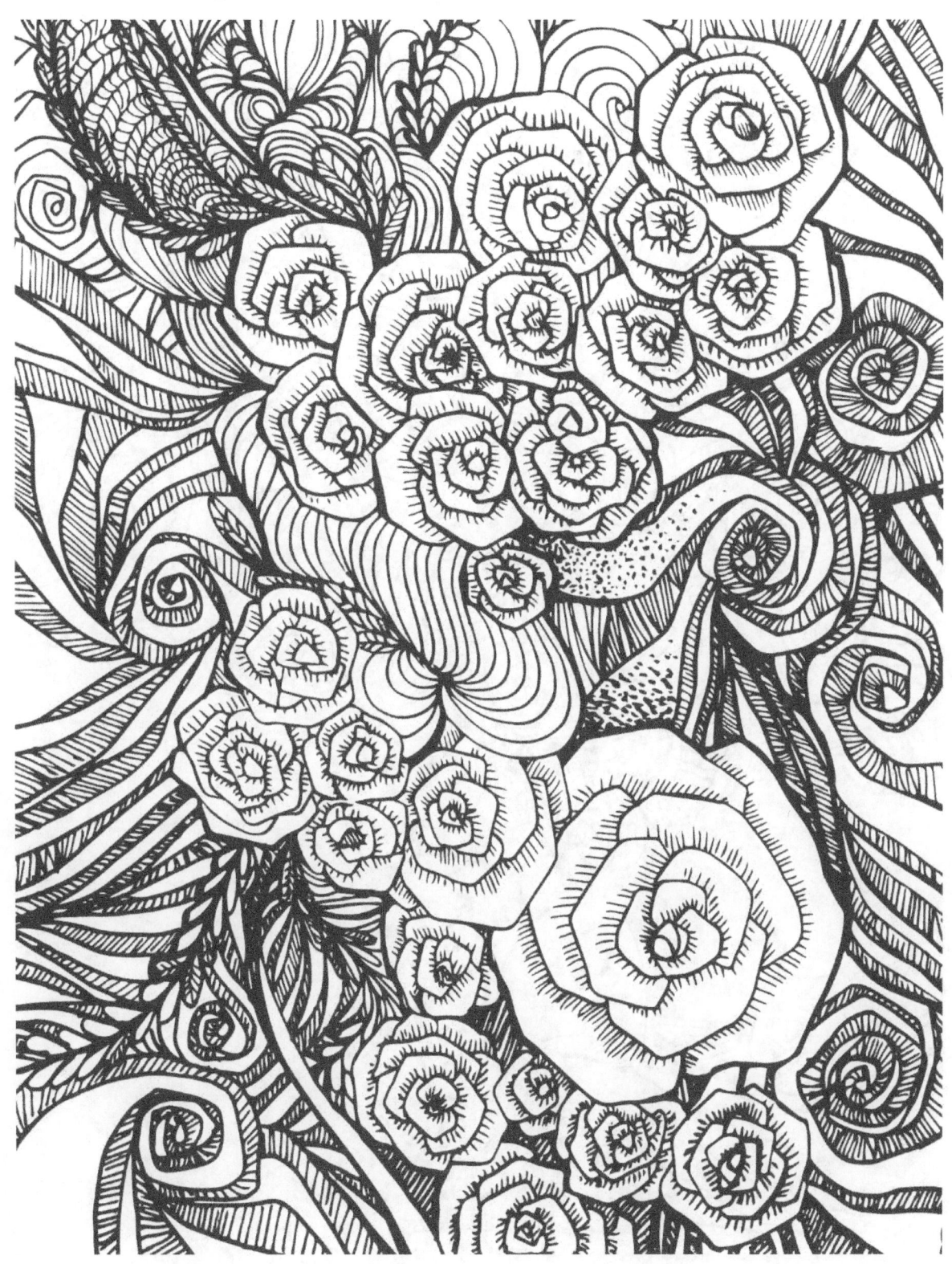

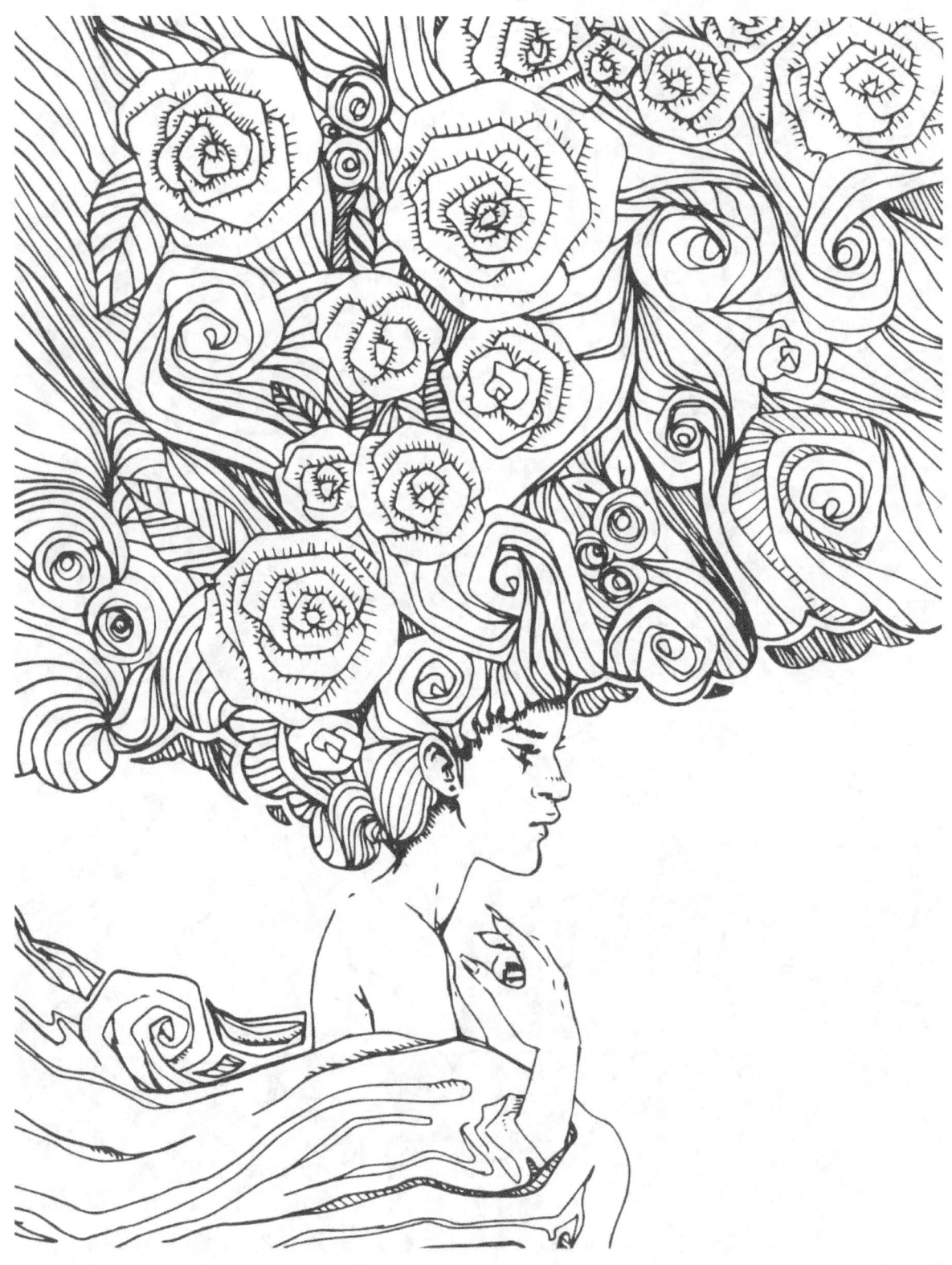

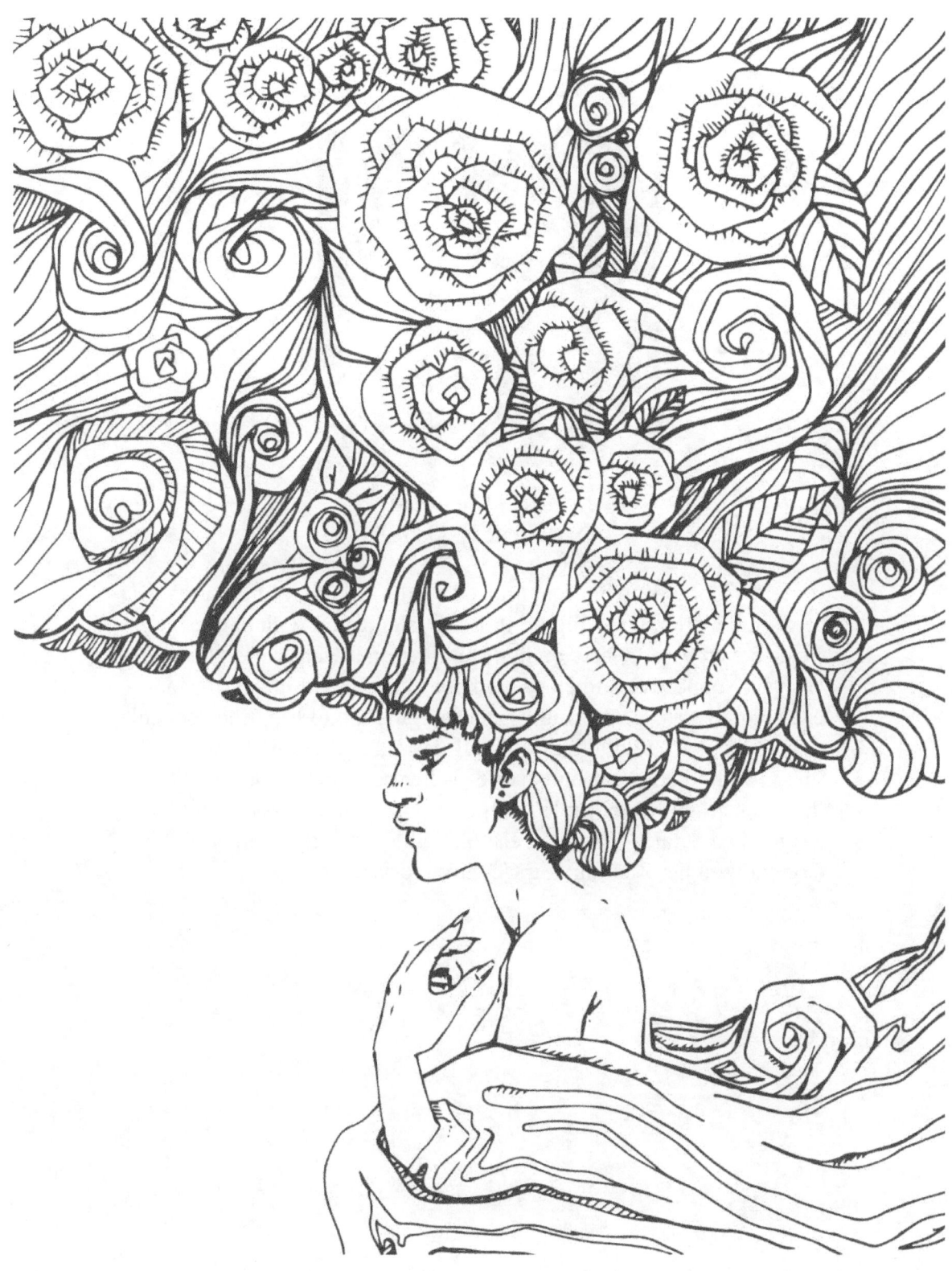

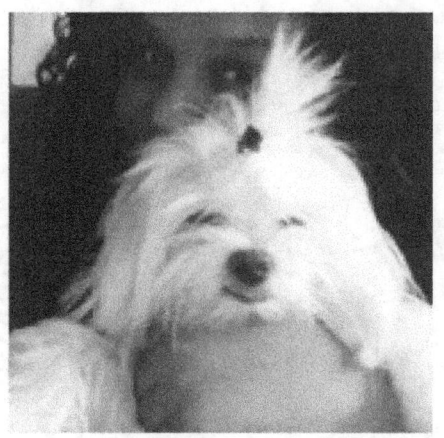

Meet the Artist
Marlene C. Cooper

Marlene Cooper was born and raised on the outskirts of the greatest city in the world. Growing up in Long Island, NY with her family, she discovered very early on her predilection towards art. Her mother was very supportive and cultivated her interest, and much of Marlene's youth was spent bringing her imagination to life. She specializes in concept art, digital painting, UI design, and graphic design. The Tranquil Mind coloring book series is her pet project come to life. She has worked for multiple independent game developers and has designed cover art for several eBooks. She currently resides in Virginia with her Zuchon dog Ceres Victoria.

www.ingramcontent.com/pod-product-compliance
Lightning Source LLC
Chambersburg PA
CBHW080708190526
45169CB00006B/2289